[fig. 001]
Shabonos, constructed of wood and palm leaves, maintaining a distance between the jungle and the community's living area.

Thresholds are anthropological invariants: they are found in every culture and in every era. Like the notions of limits and borders, they express one of humanity's fundamental relations to space.

[fig. 002]

[fig. 003]

[fig. 004]

[fig. 005]

[fig. 006]

[fig. 007]

Thresholds serve to delineate one place from another, as well as to connect them—places that have a mutual relationship of discontinuity, opposition or complementarity—and to constitute a transition from one to the other. Thresholds are always linked to the idea of crossing.

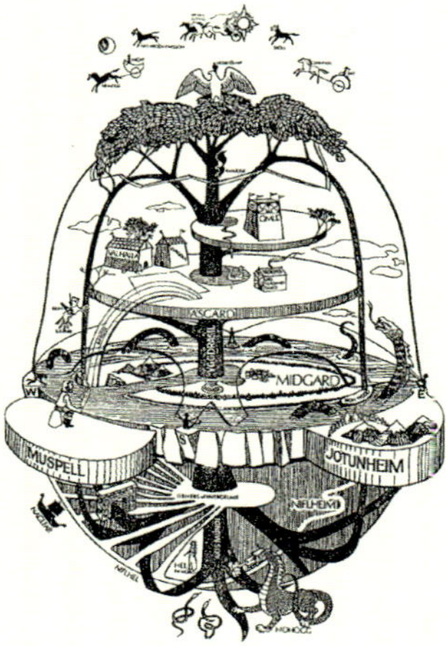

[fig. 008]
The nine worlds in Norse mythology rest on an ash tree, known as *Yggdrasil*. It represents the world tree, connecting the different parts of the universe.

[fig. 009]
Aztec mythology produced a calendar that connects time and space, designed in a cyclic manner using three systems: divinatory, solar and Venusian.

For there to be a threshold, there must therefore be at least two contiguous spaces that are the object of a distinction. The rich history of thresholds is linked to the fact that people believed for a long time that there existed spaces of different natures and statuses, governed by different laws. Before the modern concept of space, born out of the Copernican Revolution, humanity thought of spaces in the plural, often in terms of places.

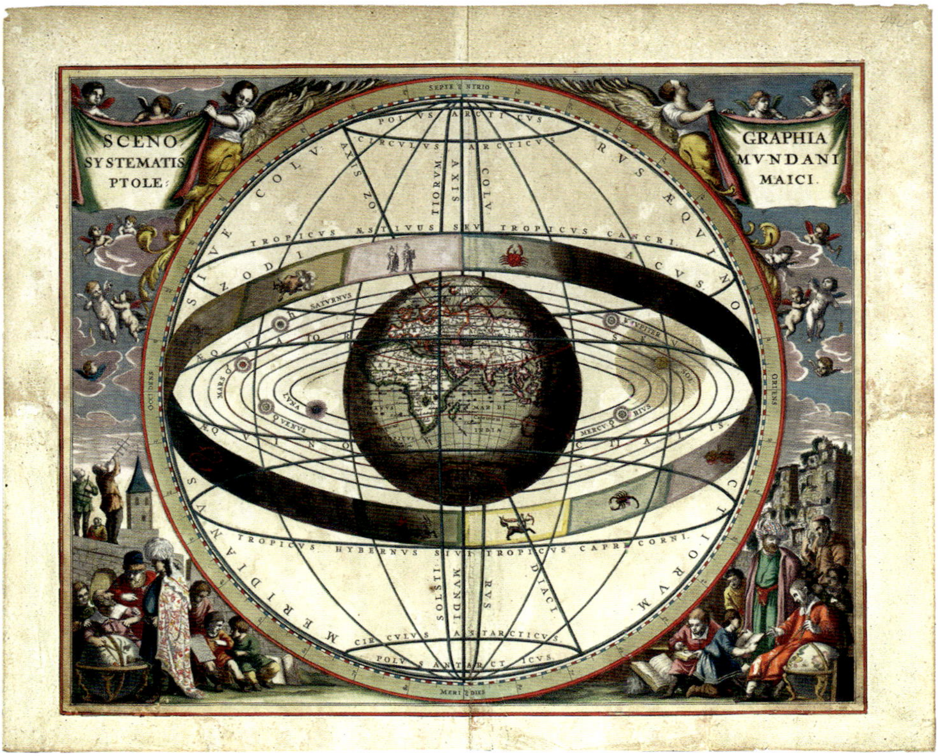

[fig. 010]

[fig. 011]
According to Descartes, the world is a spatial continuum; thresholds only exist to the extent that they are produced.

For the Ancient Greeks, for example, this topological way of thinking manifested itself not only in the distinction between the superlunary and sublunary celestial spheres but also, on earth, in the distinction between two types of place, *Topos* and *Khôra*, respectively the spatiality of every substance and the ontological sense of place.

[fig. 012]
According to Plato, the *Khôra* represents the "placeless place from which everything that is derives", undefined and ontologically related to everything within it, like a river in its bed.

[fig. 013]
Aristotle's *Topos* influenced the concept of "place" in modern European thought. It is a finite space with clear boundaries. Objects can be removed from the space in which they lie.

[fig. 014]
The threshold invites you to cross a border: it embodies both the transition and the transitional space.

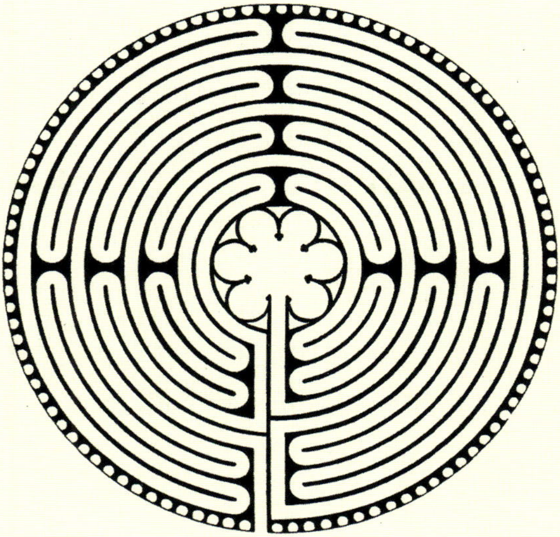

[fig. 015]
Labyrinths or *paths to Jerusalem* are meditative paths, metaphors of human existence that commit the pilgrim to a journey towards “otherness”.

The threshold refers to the experience of a transition where, most of the time, a transformation of the self takes place. It is for this reason that we find thresholds in numerous rituals, both sacred and profane.

When you're young, you always feel that life hasn't yet begun—that *life* is always scheduled to begin next week, next month, and next year, after the holidays—whenever. But then suddenly you're old and the scheduled life didn't arrive.

Douglas Coupland
Life After God

[fig. 016]

[fig. 017]
This diver has just come of age and is learning to become a man.

[fig. 018]

Crossing a threshold is often the object of a certain theatricalization and architectural dramaturgy, intended to underline the significance of the transition—hence the concept of liminality, inseparable from the concept of threshold proposed by Arnold Van Gennep, where the initiand is no longer in a state of separation, but not yet reincorporated into society: it is this inbetween stage that is embodied and symbolized by the threshold.

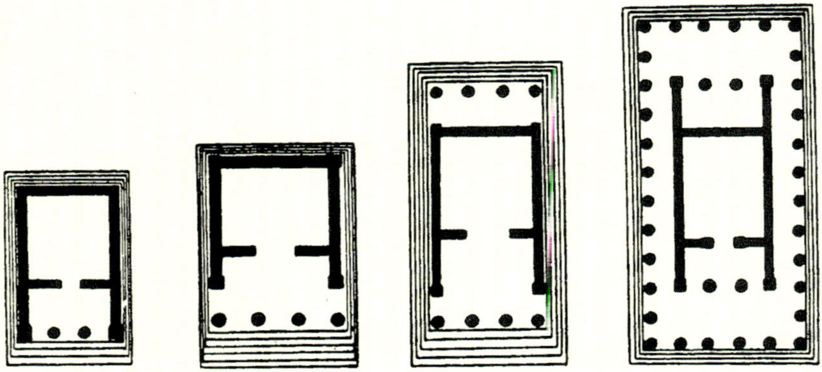

[fig. 019]
Walks take place outside the Greek temple, which houses the central core or cella built as the "impenetrable home of the gods".

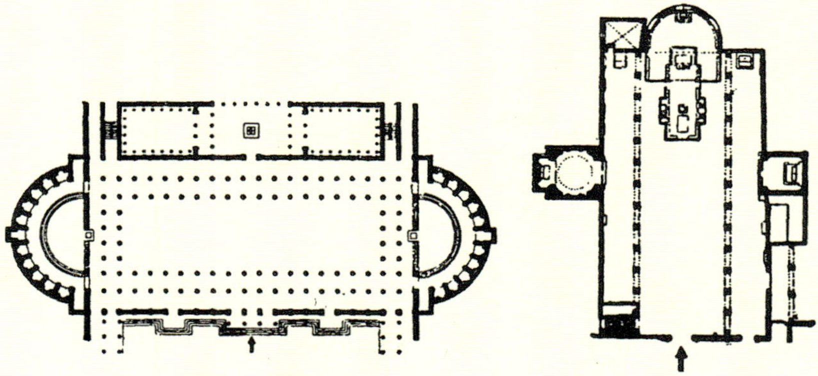

[fig. 020]
In contrast, on Roman basilicas the colonnades are found inside, designed to be inhabited by man.

Thresholds always have a width, whether symbolic or physical, whether an invisible line or an intermediate space. It is within this width that changes and transformations occur. In this sense, thresholds always have both a spatial and a temporal dimension.

[fig. 021]

[fig. 022]

It should be noted that thresholds are often imagined to be unidirectional, whereas it is in fact possible to pass through them in both directions. In general, we have tended to move from the profane to the sacred, from the private to the public (in Ancient Greece and Rome) and from the public to the private (in the Europe of the 18th century onwards)—always from the lesser to the more significant.

[fig. 023]
At the main entrance to Japanese sacred places, ample space is given as protection from demons and evil spirits.

[fig. 024]
An eruv is a symbolic border, an enclosure in which certain rules from the Talmud and the Torah can be breached.

Impossible to distinguish the mass of the church from that of neighbouring secular buildings. The stranger passes it by. The inconspicuous door, often only a curtain, is the secret gate for the initiate. A single step takes him from the humble of dirty courtyards into the pure solitude of a tall, whitewashed church interior.

Walter Benjamin & Asja Lacis
Naples

[fig. 025]

[fig. 026]

[fig. 027]

[fig. 028]
Street: space for public opinion and to gather an audience.

[fig. 029]

The threshold between the public and private spheres does not connect two spaces of different natures—or which are deemed to be such—but instead links two spaces with different statuses that the threshold ranks in terms of superiority. We are always obliged to leave one in order to access the other. This distinction, equally useful from a spatial standpoint, has evolved constantly, right to the present day.

ATHENIAN AGORA
2ND - CENTURY A.D.
SACRED GATE
DIPYLON GATE
STOA POIKILE
ERIDANOS RIVER
(HADRIAN STREET)
(ST. PHILIP)
ROYAL STOA
BASILICA
SHOP and HOUSES
ARSENAL
STOA of ZEUS
ALTAR of the 12 GODS
STREET OF THE PANATHENAIA
HEPHAISTEION
APOLLO PATROOS
TEMPLE of ARES
MONOPTEROS
METROON
ODEION of AGRIPPA
BOULEUTERION
ALTAR OF ZEUS AGORAIOS ?
EPONYMOUS HEROES
BEMA
STOA of ATTALOS
KOLONOS AGORAIOS
THOLOS
S.W TEMPLE
CIVIC OFFICES
STRATEGEION ?
LATRINE
MIDDLE STOA
LIBRARY of PANTAINOS
EAST BUILDING
SOUTH SQUARE
S.W FOUNTAIN HOUSE
RECTANGULAR PERIBOLOS
SOUTH STOA II
PIRAEUS GATE
NYMPHAION
SOUTH STOA I
S.E. STOA
S.E. TEMPLE
S.E. FOUNTAIN HOUSE
MINT
SHRINE
BATHS
HOUSES
PRE-ROMAN HOUSES
200 meters
ACROPOLIS

[fig. 030]

[fig. 031]
In Shanghai, the habit of appropriating public spaces endures, despite changes in modern towns.

For a long time, the private domain represented the sphere that must be left behind in order to access the *res publica*, the sphere of political activity, where recognition among peers fostered an egalitarian and liberating space. This was the case in Ancient Greece and Rome, where the home was considered a prepolitical space, lacking the constituent values of the free man.

It is with respect to this multiple significance of the public realm that the term *private*, in its original privative sense, has meaning. To live an entirely private life means above all to be deprived of things essential to a truly human life [...] The privation of privacy lies in the absence of others.

Hannah Arendt
The Human Condition

[fig. 032]

[fig. 033]

This devaluation of the private domain changed with the development of Christianity, a religion that privatized one's relationship with the divine. Merely talking about the meaning of the law no longer sufficed: it was necessary to internalize it, embody it, and live and experience it in one's inner self. However, it was only in the 18th century, with the advent of the nation state, that the subordination of the private domain to the public sphere was inverted.

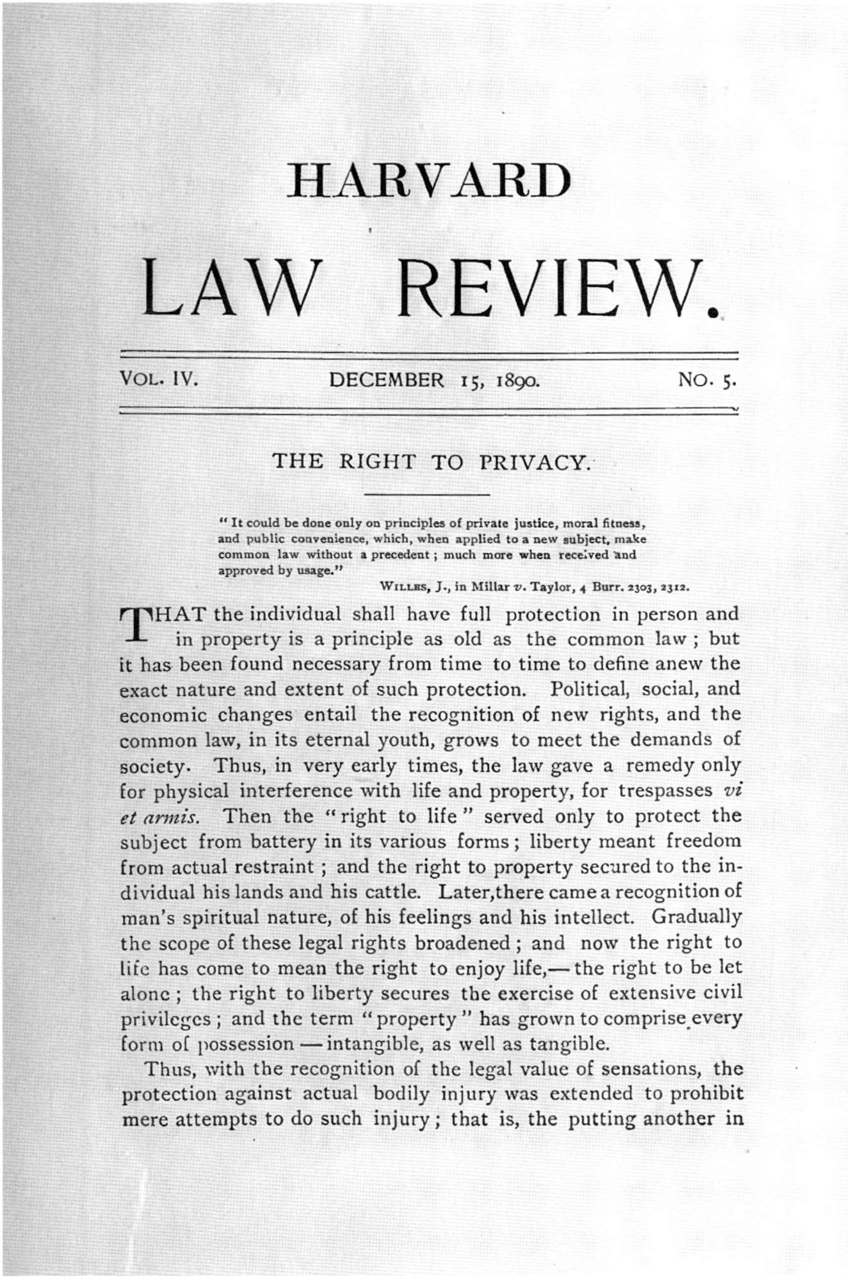

HARVARD LAW REVIEW.

VOL. IV. DECEMBER 15, 1890. NO. 5.

THE RIGHT TO PRIVACY.

"It could be done only on principles of private justice, moral fitness, and public convenience, which, when applied to a new subject, make common law without a precedent; much more when received and approved by usage."

WILLES, J., in Millar *v.* Taylor, 4 Burr. 2303, 2312.

THAT the individual shall have full protection in person and in property is a principle as old as the common law; but it has been found necessary from time to time to define anew the exact nature and extent of such protection. Political, social, and economic changes entail the recognition of new rights, and the common law, in its eternal youth, grows to meet the demands of society. Thus, in very early times, the law gave a remedy only for physical interference with life and property, for trespasses *vi et armis.* Then the "right to life" served only to protect the subject from battery in its various forms; liberty meant freedom from actual restraint; and the right to property secured to the individual his lands and his cattle. Later, there came a recognition of man's spiritual nature, of his feelings and his intellect. Gradually the scope of these legal rights broadened; and now the right to life has come to mean the right to enjoy life,— the right to be let alone; the right to liberty secures the exercise of extensive civil privileges; and the term "property" has grown to comprise every form of possession — intangible, as well as tangible.

Thus, with the recognition of the legal value of sensations, the protection against actual bodily injury was extended to prohibit mere attempts to do such injury; that is, the putting another in

[fig. 034]

[fig. 035]

[fig. 036]

With the emergence of the social question and attempts to regulate and administer, politically, everything that formerly belonged to the private domain, the personal and the intimate became protected and valorized as the expression of a modern subjectivity to be defended.

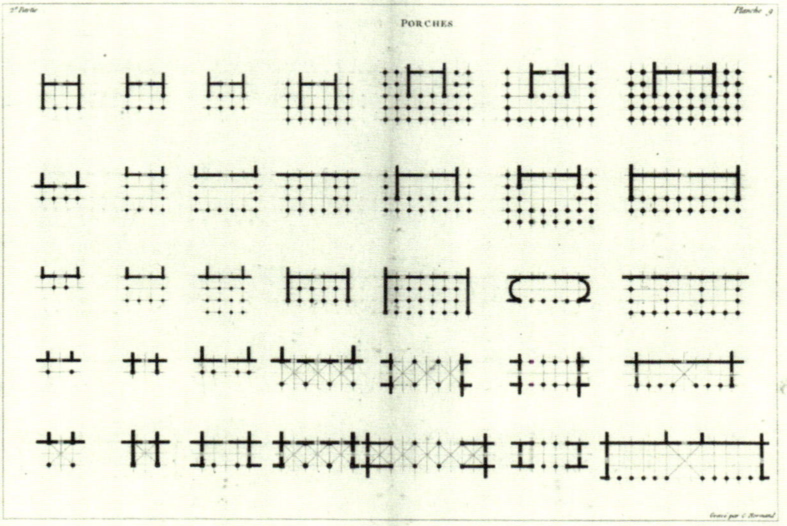

[fig. 037]

[fig. 038]
Between inwardness and opening up to the outside: an inventive solution of sliding walls and mirrors lets Marie-Antoinette create her *boudoir*.

From this point on, the home became the natural location of one's inner life and its orchestration: the vestibule, antechamber, boudoir and bedroom are all spaces whose accessibility is carefully defined and controlled.

[fig. 039]

Ultimately, this overvalorization of the private domain, to the detriment of the public sphere, has led to the erosion of the relationship between the two. The home is an inward-looking entity, which no longer needs to relate to the outside—or to communicate with it via thresholds.

[fig. 040]

Walter Benjamin underlined this solipsism present in the living environments of the 19th century bourgeoisie conceived as cocoons that would protect their occupants from the outside world that capitalism was steadily transforming.

[fig. 041]
In the 18th century, living spaces were also spaces for work.

[fig. 042]
The *Cubicle*, designed by Robert Propst as a work space adapted and adjustable to the needs of workers, has surpassed the intentions of its inventor.

[fig. 043]
Parking space, linked directly with the kitchen, expresses modernist perfection.

With the advent of big cities, the need to isolate oneself became a vital concern; the threshold once again underwent significant changes, but tended to be reduced to a functional sequence, gradually becoming devoid of all symbolic meaning, and the associated scenography.

[fig. 044]

This trend has merely been confirmed—and indeed has accelerated—with the fragmentation of urban spaces, the increasing specialization of living and work spaces, and the gradual replacement of public space by space for crowds.

[fig. 045]

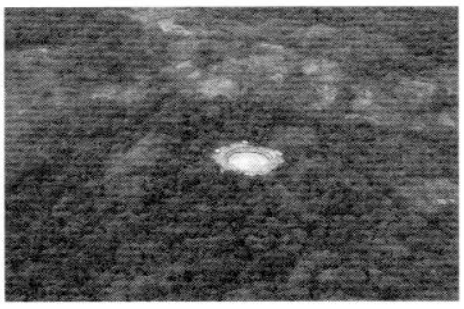

[fig. 001]
Yanomami tribal village with surrounding gardens, Watoriktheri, Brazil

[fig. 002]
The porch of Howard Phillips Lovecraft's House, 10 Barnes Street, Providence, Rhode Island, USA

[fig. 003]
Engawa in a Japanese house, Nagano, Japan

[fig. 004]
Erik Korshagen, *Architect's own summerhouse*, Rørvig, Denmark, 1960

[fig. 005]
Old Wardour Castle, Wiltshire, UK

[fig. 006]
Ettore Sottsass Jr., *Metafore, C'è sempre una porta attraverso la quale incontri il tuo amore,* 1976, Dolomiti

[fig. 007]
Footbridge on the Indus River, Pakistan

[fig. 008]
Representation of the nine worlds of Norse mythology

[fig. 009]
Aztec calendar

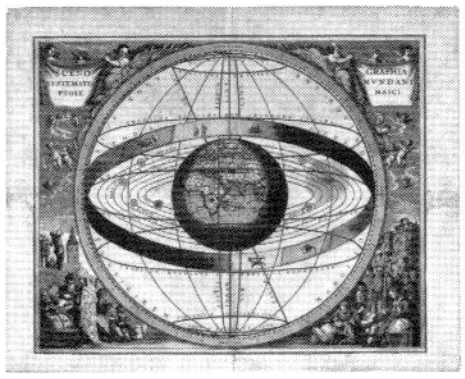

[fig. 010]
Johannes van Loon, *Reproduction of the geocentric system of Ptolemy*, 1660/1661

[fig. 011]
Superstudio, *A Journey from A to B*, 1969

[fig. 012]
Aerial view of Red River, north of Bonham, Fannin County, northeast Texas, USA

[fig. 013]
Mission Apollo 11, Buzz Aldrin on the moon in 1969

[fig. 014]
Weightlifters

[fig. 015]
Labyrinth of the Cathedral of Chartres, France, extracted from *Gothique-Architecture Universelle*, 1968

[fig. 016]
Photogram from *Diamond Island*, directed by Davy Chou, 2016

[fig. 017]
Gol land diving, Pentecost Island, Vanuatu

[fig. 018]
Purification baths in the holy water of the sacred source of Tirta Empul, Bali, Indonesia

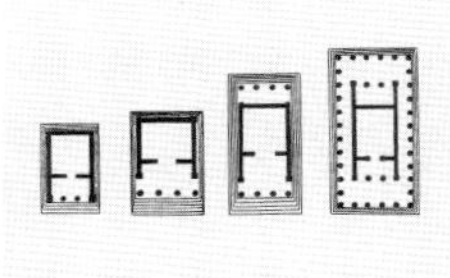

[fig. 019]
Typological evolution of the Greek temple, extracted from *Saper vedere l'architettura*, 1948

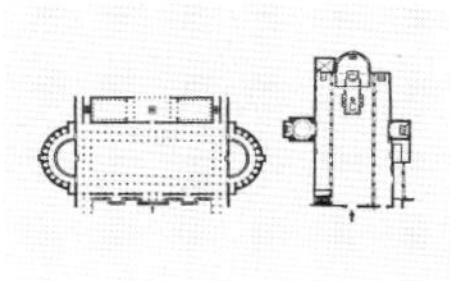

[fig. 020]
Plan of the Basilica Ulpia, built in Rome between 107 and 112 AD., extracted from *Saper vedere l'architettura*, 1948

[fig. 021]
Nuttinee Karnchanaporn, *The threshold of a Thaihouse*, Samut Songkhram, 2016

[fig. 022]
The mortuary Temple of Hatshepsut, Luxor Governorate, Egypt

[fig. 023]
Byōbuura Gogakusan Tanjō-in Zentsū-ji temple, Kagawa, Japan

[fig. 024]
Eruv at Tower of David, Old Jerusalem, Israel

[fig. 025]
A view of Dubaï, UAE

[fig. 026]
Portal of the north arm of the transept of the Notre-Dame de la Treille Cathedral, Lille, France

[fig. 027]
Dompilze, former bus stop, Cologne, Germany

[fig. 028]
Women's March on Washington, USA, January 21, 2017

[fig. 029]
Two boys seated outside their home, Antigua and Barbuda

[fig. 030]
General plan of the Athenian Agora in the 2nd century AD.

[fig. 031]
Sensual City Studio, Shanghai, *Mindwalks*, 2016

[fig. 032]
Myr Muratet, *Aménagement Sauvage—Porte d'Aubervilliers*
2016

[fig. 033]
Lia Nalbantidou, *Untitled (NALBW02 00808 96)*
from the series *The Secure, Private Domain of my Home (1996—2001)—Zero to Five*

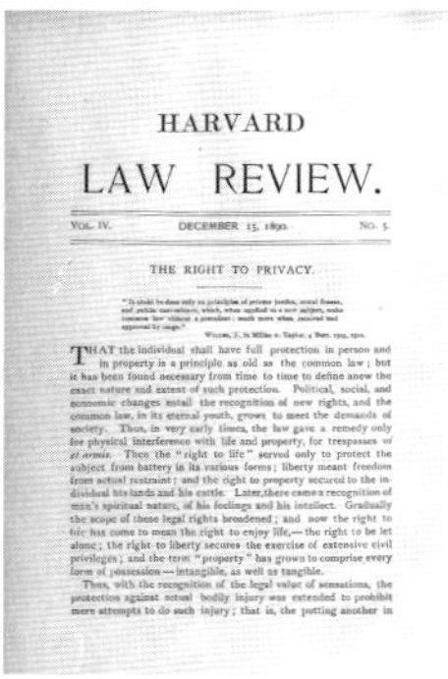

HARVARD

LAW REVIEW.

VOL. IV. DECEMBER 15, 1890. NO. 5.

THE RIGHT TO PRIVACY.

THAT the individual shall have full protection in person and in property is a principle as old as the common law; but it has been found necessary from time to time to define anew the exact nature and extent of such protection. Political, social, and economic changes entail the recognition of new rights, and the common law, in its eternal youth, grows to meet the demands of society. Thus, in very early times, the law gave a remedy only for physical interference with life and property, for trespasses *vi et armis*. Then the "right to life" served only to protect the subject from battery in its various forms; liberty meant freedom from actual restraint; and the right to property secured to the individual his lands and his cattle. Later, there came a recognition of man's spiritual nature, of his feelings and his intellect. Gradually the scope of these legal rights broadened; and now the right to life has come to mean the right to enjoy life,—the right to be let alone; the right to liberty secures the exercise of extensive civil privileges; and the term "property" has grown to comprise every form of possession—intangible, as well as tangible.

Thus, with the recognition of the legal value of sensations, the protection against actual bodily injury was extended to prohibit mere attempts to do such injury; that is, the putting another in

[fig. 034]
Samuel D. Warren
and Louis D. Brandeis,
"The Right to Privacy"
extracted from *Harvard Law Review*, Nº 5, 1890

[fig. 035]
Californian blinds

[fig. 036]
Paris by night, Paris, France, 2017

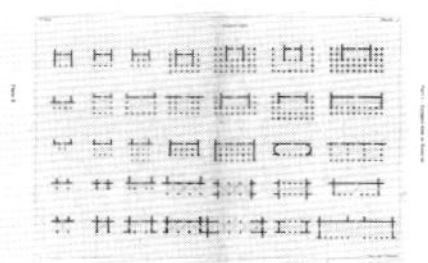

[fig. 037]
Porch typology board extracted from
Jean-Nicolas-Louis Durand Graphic Portion of the Lectures on Architecture, 1821

[fig. 038]
Cabinet des glaces mouvantes, Petit Trianon, Versailles, France

[fig. 039]
University residence,
Coles County, Illinois, USA

[fig. 040]
Teenage room in the 1960s

[fig. 041]
Bookbinding workshop, engraving extracted from the *Diderot & d'Alembert encyclopaedia*, 1751—1772

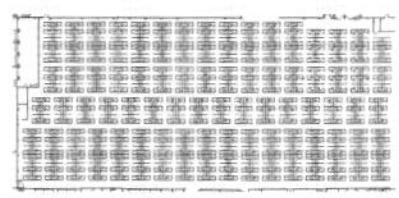

[fig. 042]
Office floor plan showing repetitive, regimented cubicles

[fig. 043]
Pierre Koenig, *Bailey House*,
Case Study House #21,
Los Angeles, California,
USA, 1958

[fig. 044]
Suburbs, Houston,
Texas, USA

[fig. 045]
Interchange project
in northeast Mecklenburg
County, Charlotte,
North Carolina, USA

[fig. 046]

[fig. 047]

[fig. 048]

Thresholds do not seem to have disappeared, and yet they are in fact dead. In the early 20th century, a profound transformation was underway that would cause thresholds to lose their *raison d'être*. Increasingly specialized spaces proliferated, but there was no longer any need to interconnect them as spaces offering distinct experiences.

WARNING
This door is only
to be used for
entering and
exiting

[fig. 049]

[fig. 050]

By presenting the simultaneity of (real) confinement and (apparent) openness as a leitmotif of the International Style, architecture killed thresholds by eliminating the question of how the inside and outside should be connected.

[fig. 051]

[fig. 052]

Absolute transparency became a synonym for truth and emancipation, which nothing should impede, to the point of purging interiors of all opaqueness. Glass was viewed as a purifying material: a tool to enable the voluntary shedding of the apparel that obscured access to oneself and to the world.

The face of the earth would be much altered if brick architecture were ousted everywhere by glass architecture. It would be as if the earth were adorned with sparkling jewels and enamels. Such glory is unimaginable. [...] We should then have a paradise on earth, and no need to watch in longing expectation for the paradise in heaven.

Paul Scheerbart
Glass Architecture

[fig. 053]

[fig. 054]

The invention of artificial lighting and air conditioning would radically transform the fundamental relationship that architecture previously maintained with light and air. Buildings no longer had to be oriented according to the sun or the wind, to be able to open up for purposes of ventilation, or to adapt to seasonal variations in temperature. Buildings became hermetic envelopes designed to contain a constant, controlled environment.

[fig. 055]
Projects like *Biosphere 2* or the *Eden Project* have tried to address the difficulties associated with controlling of an artificial ecosystem.

[fig. 056]

[fig. 057]

It is no surprise that the emergence of glass architecture coincided with the development of new environmental control techniques: transparency was leveraged to create a new relationship with the outside—a purely visual relationship that turned interior spaces into bubbles cut off from the world, but open to the gazes of all.

[fig. 058]

In a quite different sense, the development of the building envelope heralded the emergence of an architecture of interiority, indifferent to its exterior.

[fig. 059]
The owner of this house turned down an offer of $1m from property developers: they were forced to construct their shopping center around the hundred-year-old building.

Closure, mutual exclusion and a return to the object were the watchwords of a self-centred and decontextualized architecture—a fitting reflection of globalization.

[fig. 060]

Today, there is no need to interconnect spaces. The reason is simple: knowing and understanding how we fit into space has become obsolete. Thresholds have also been dented by the unprecedented growth and intensification of mobility, whether residential, professional or touristic.

[fig. 061]

Day-to-day city life within the modern metropolis now appears to be nothing more than the juxtaposition of never-ending transitions between specialized and exclusive environments on the one hand and a space of hypermobility that is neither delineated nor defined on the other.

Le Capitalisme
CAPITALISM
Nous vous gouvernons
WE RULE YOU
Nous vous trompons
WE FOOL YOU
Nous vous fusillons
WE SHOOT AT YOU
WE EAT FOR YOU
Nous mangenons pour vous
WE WORK FOR ALL
Nous travaillons pour vous tous
WE FEED ALL
Nous vous nourissons tous
PYRAMID OF CAPITALIST SYSTEM
La Pyramide du systéme capitaliste
ISSUED BY NEDELJKOVICH, BRASHICH AND KUHARICH.
Copyrighted 1911 by The International Pub. Co., 1747 W. 25th St., Cleveland, O., U. S. A.

[fig. 062]

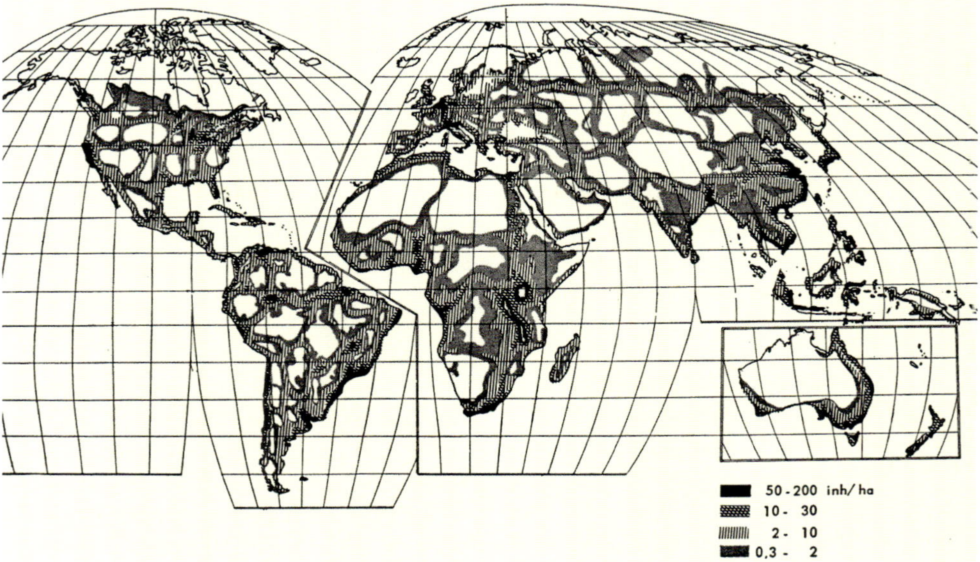

[fig. 063]
Ecumenopolis: a planet-wide city continues to be planned as "the inevitable city of the future".

The everyday space of our dreams now resembles an overlapping jumble of philosopher Peter Sloterdijk's bubbles and foams. The earth itself seems to have shrunk under the effect of a globalization that enables us to travel around the world without stopping—a world that has become hyperspatial, but which sweeps the otherness of places under the carpet when it is deemed a hindrance to mobility.

[fig. 064]

[fig. 065]

In order to become accessible and attract all those who pass by, places have to give up part of their identity and become more commonplace. Retaining just enough exoticism to justify venturing in, they exhibit increasingly generic traits that enable everyone to find their bearings and feel sufficiently at home.

[fig. 066]

[fig. 067]

The market economy presumes the existence of workers without attachments who are capable of leaving places and their history behind. If globalization is indeed, as Zygmund Bauman claimed, a war against space, this is first and foremost because space is perceived as a constraint and no longer as a resource.

[fig. 068]

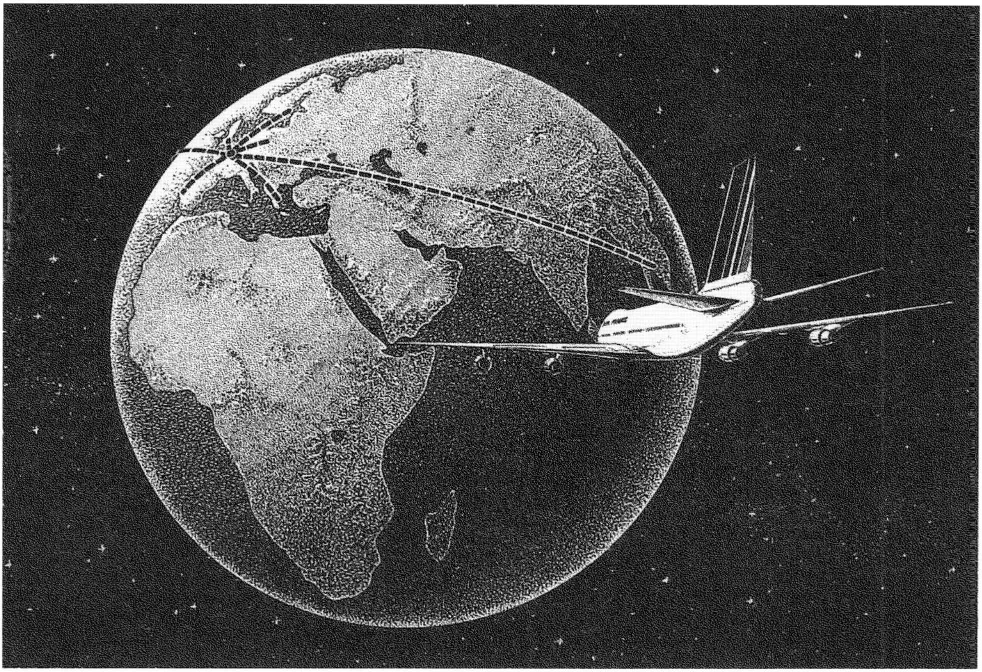

[fig. 069]

The obsession with mobility reduces every journey to a simple connection from point A to point B. Now, when travelling, all that counts is the destination, while the trials and tribulations of the journey to get there must be reduced to a strict minimum.

He could see no horizon other than that of metal against sky, stretching out to almost uniform grayness, and he knew it was so over all the land surface of the planet. There was scarcely any motion to be seen—a few pleasure craft lazed against the sky—but all the busy traffic of billions of men was going on [...] beneath the metal skin of the world.

Isaac Asimov
Foundation

[fig. 070]

[fig. 071]

[fig. 072]

Thresholds have become impediments to a hypermobile society that lurches between accelerating and shuffling along. This is why, today, thresholds subsist solely in forms relating to safety and security: gates, queues and security checks.

[fig. 073]

We no longer pay any particular attention to space. The generalized use of screens and smartphones has only reinforced the obsolescence of thresholds. Travel has become atopic.

[fig. 074]

Geolocation tools have eradicated our sense of place, the notion of paying attention to the landscape, and the use of schematic maps. To reach our destination, all we have to do is turn left or right.

[fig. 075]

[fig. 076]
The move to paperless communication systems has resulted in the construction of enormous underwater networks.

Journeys from one point in space to another are no longer experiences, and indeed are not even felt as lived moments any more: rapidity and instant connection are now the objectives du jour, along with the reduction of space to its bare minimum.

[fig. 077]

[fig. 078]
Virtual reality allows the revival of architectural utopia.

As it gradually loses its quality as a place where life flourishes, space also loses all attractiveness and all density. Its only reality is the data it is composed of. In concrete terms, the utopia of mobility is now the utopia of teleportation.

[fig. 079]

[fig. 046]
Smoker in front of his office

[fig. 047]
Hostile architecture

[fig. 048]
Revolving door

[fig. 049]
Warning message

[fig. 050]
Philip Johnson, *Glass House*, New Canaan, Connecticut, USA, 1949

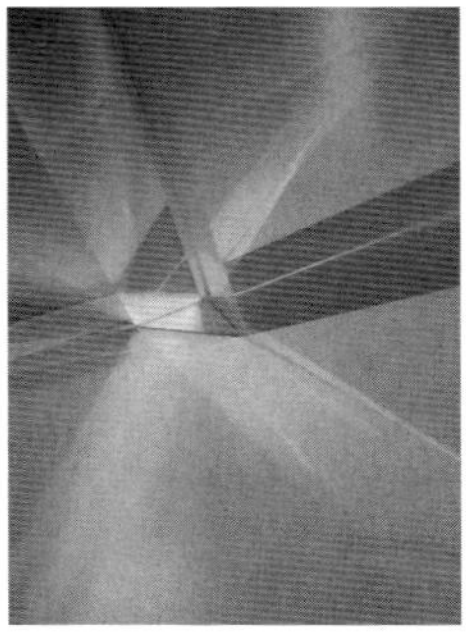

[fig. 051]
Sensual City Studio, study model for a luminaire, 2017

[fig. 052]
Man looking out the window

[fig. 053]
Pipilotti Rist, *The Innocent Collection*, 1985. Installation view, *Pipilotti Rist. Your saliva is my diving suit in the ocean of pain*, Kunsthaus, Zurich, Switzerland, 2016. Photo: Lena Huber

[fig. 054]
Air conditioners on a facade on Park Avenue, New York, USA

[fig. 055]
Alberto Giuliani, *Biosphere to preserve the forest biodiversity in UK*, from the series *Surviving Humanity* started in March 2016

[fig. 056]
Joseph Paxton, *Crystal Palace*, London, UK, 1851

[fig. 057]
Photogram from *The Touchables*, directed by Robert Freeman, 1968

Death

[fig. 058]
Reflections, Shanghai, China, 2008

[fig. 059]
Edith Macefield's house, Seattle, Washington, USA

[fig. 060]
Moving truck

[fig. 061]
Mall, Dubaï, UAE

[fig. 062]
Pyramid of Capitalist System, an American cartoon caricature critical of capitalism, 1911

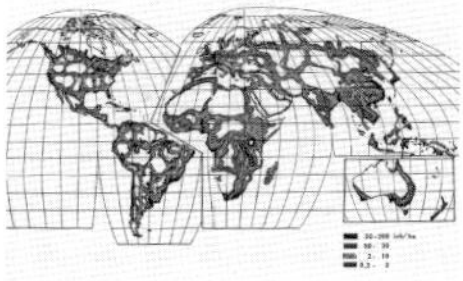

[fig. 063]
Constantinos A. Doxiadis, *Ecumenopolis at the end of the 21st century*, 1968

[fig. 064]
O'Hare International Airport, Chicago, Illinois, USA

[fig. 065]
Billboard, Shanghai, China, 2013

[fig. 066]
Trading room

[fig. 067]
Man on a platform

[fig. 068]
Billboard, Route 66, USA

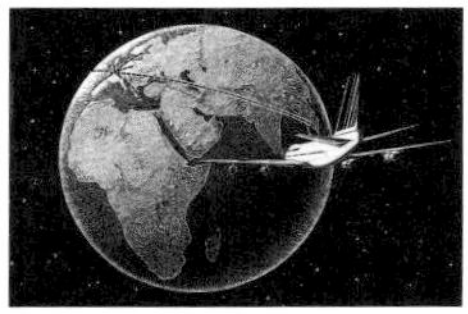

[fig. 069]
Air France commercial (detail), 1983

[fig. 070]
Render of Delft Hyperloop Atlas prototype

[fig. 071]
Customs agency in Thônex-Vallard, between France and Switzerland

[fig. 072]
Security checkpoints, Sea-Tac Airport, Seattle-Tacoma, Washington, USA

[fig. 073]
Aram Bartholl, *Map, Taipei, 2010. Public installation.*
Photo: Chang-Chih Chen

[fig. 074]
GPS on a smartphone

[fig. 075]
Telephone operators, Seattle, Washington, USA

[fig. 076]
Optic cable landing site, Guam, USA

[fig. 077]
Marenostrum supercomputer, managed and hosted by Barcelona Supercomputing Center, Barcelona, Spain

[fig. 078]
Space Popular, *The Glass Chain*, London, UK, 2017

[fig. 079]
Photogram from *Philadelphia Experiment,* directed by Stewart Raffill, 1984

[fig. 080]

[fig. 081]

[fig. 082]

While it is too late to try to revive old, moribund thresholds, it is absolutely necessary to invent new ones. If we look closely, we see that city dwellers develop strategies to counteract the pressure that is constantly pushing us towards the undefined. New rituals are being established at home, in the office, in the supermarket, on the street.

[fig. 083]

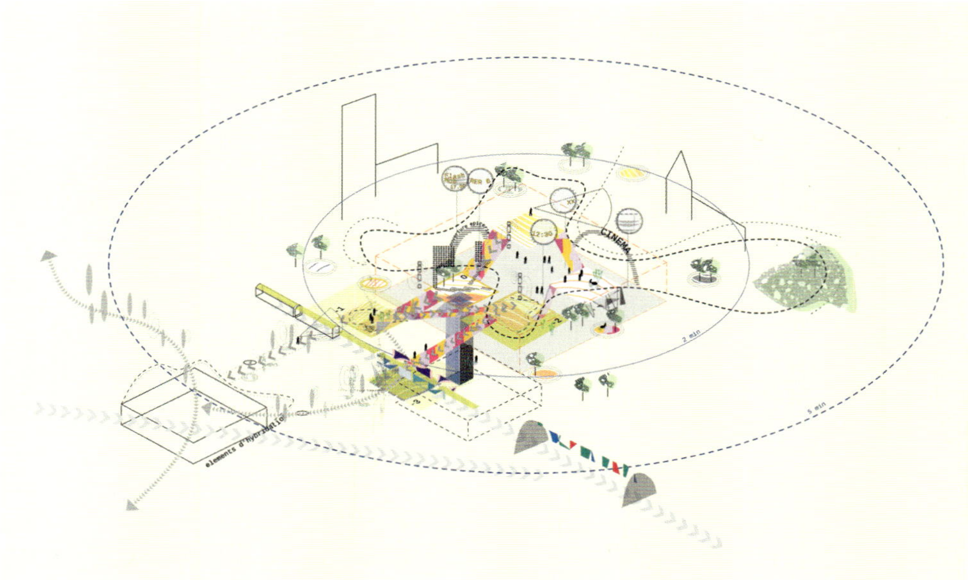

[fig. 084]

These new thresholds correspond more closely to the characteristics of the contemporary metropolis, marked by a succession of ambiences—that are becoming increasingly distinct from one another—and by generalized mobility that nevertheless manages to encompass each individual's personal wanderings.

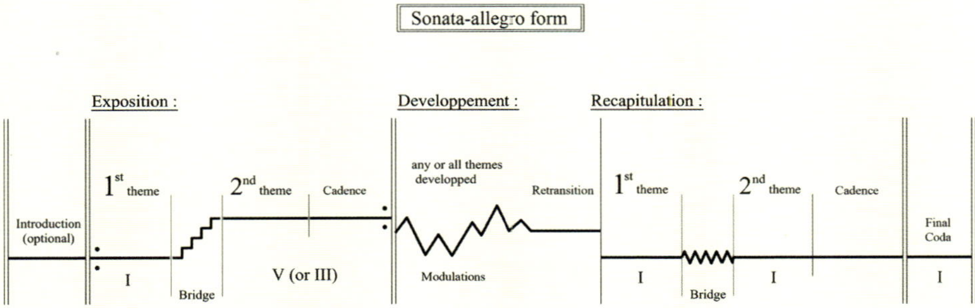

[fig. 085]
In the sonata form, transitions are the unstable episodes that produce impetus and directionality.

The inspiration is no longer to be found in the spatial arts, but instead must be sought elsewhere. It can be found in music, in particular, where space exists only through the deployment of sound in time.

[fig. 086]

This space is heard and felt, rather than seen. Here, the threshold may only be the duration of a single vibration, but is capable of linking two musical sequences with quite different emotional tones.

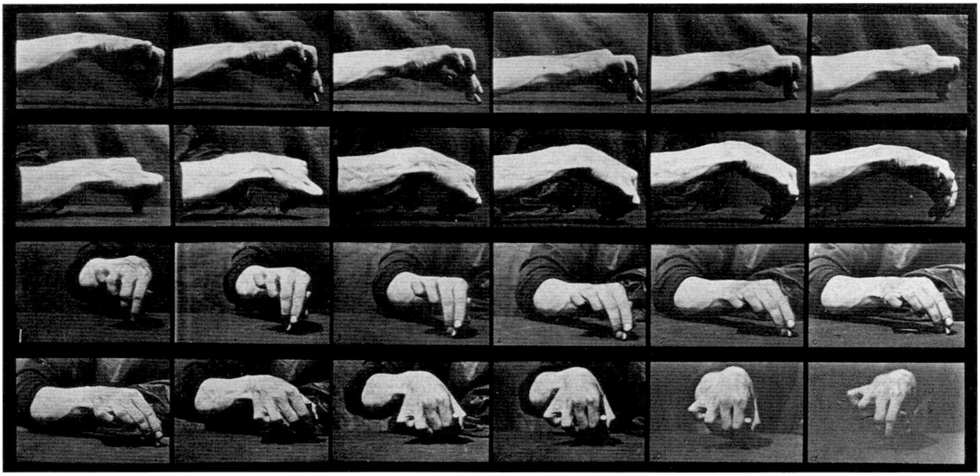

[fig. 087]

[fig. 088]

[fig. 089]

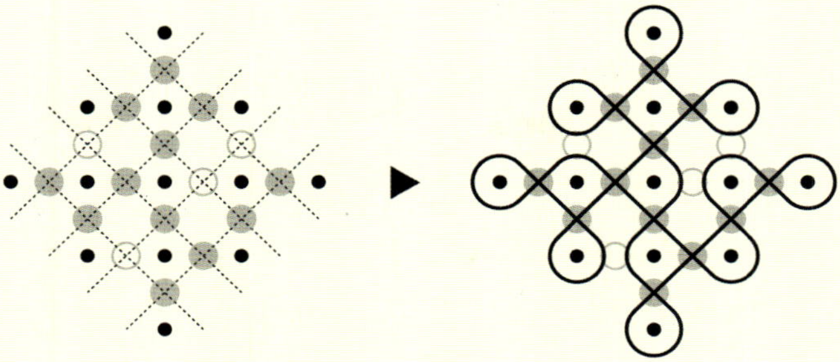

Fig. 7. Setting shapes at intersections (●: crossing, ○: uncrossing).

[fig. 090]
Kolam are the geometric powder or rice patterns made every day at the entrances to houses and businesses in southern India to bring prosperity.

I have tried several times to think of an apartment in which there would be a useless room, absolutely and intentionally useless. [...] For all my efforts, I found it impossible to follow this idea through to the end. Language itself, seemingly, proved unsuited to describing this nothing, this void, as if we could only speak of what is full, useful and functional.

Georges Perec
Species of spaces

[fig. 091]

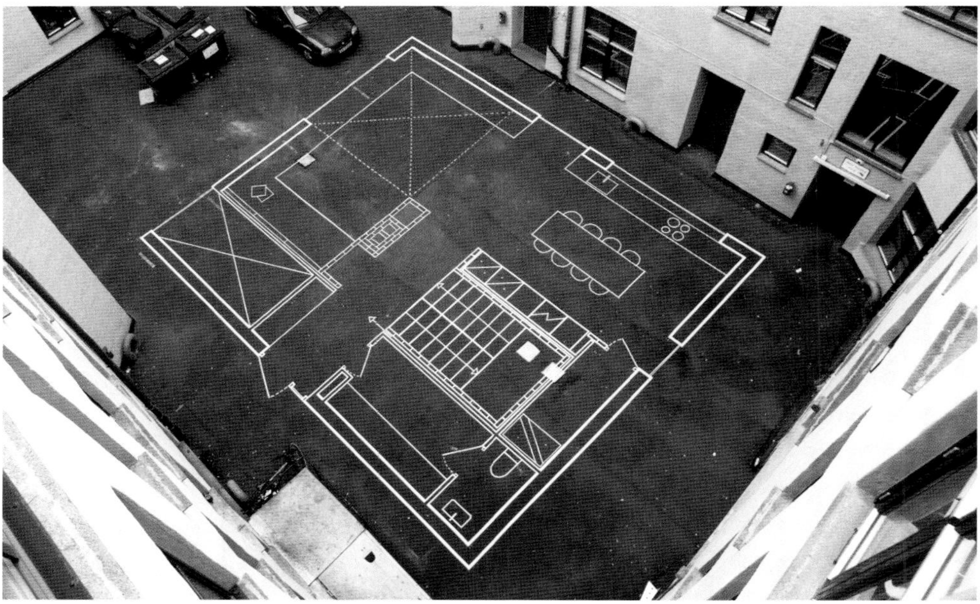

[fig. 092]

[fig. 093]

These new thresholds go hand in hand with the transition from urban planning based on geometry to urban planning based on atmospheres. It is no longer about joining together spaces of different types or statuses, but rather a question of connecting ambiences.

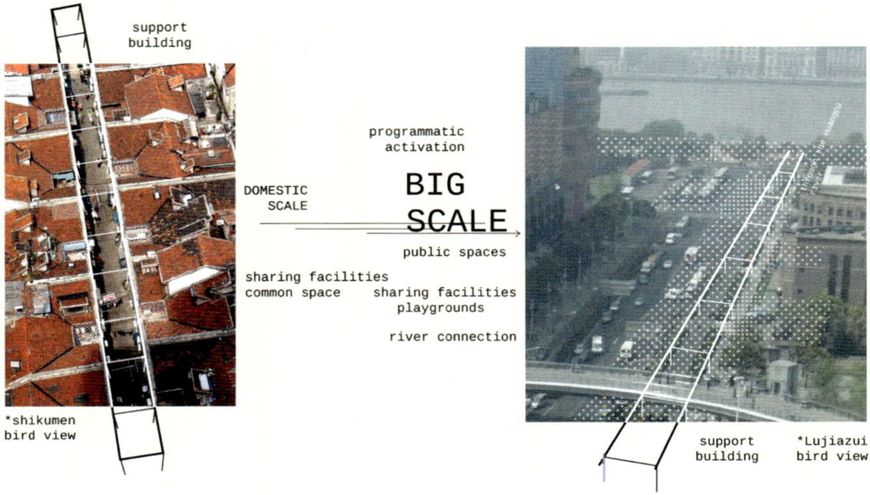

[fig. 094]
The domestic scale of the *Lilongs* was transposed onto that of the generic Chinese town.

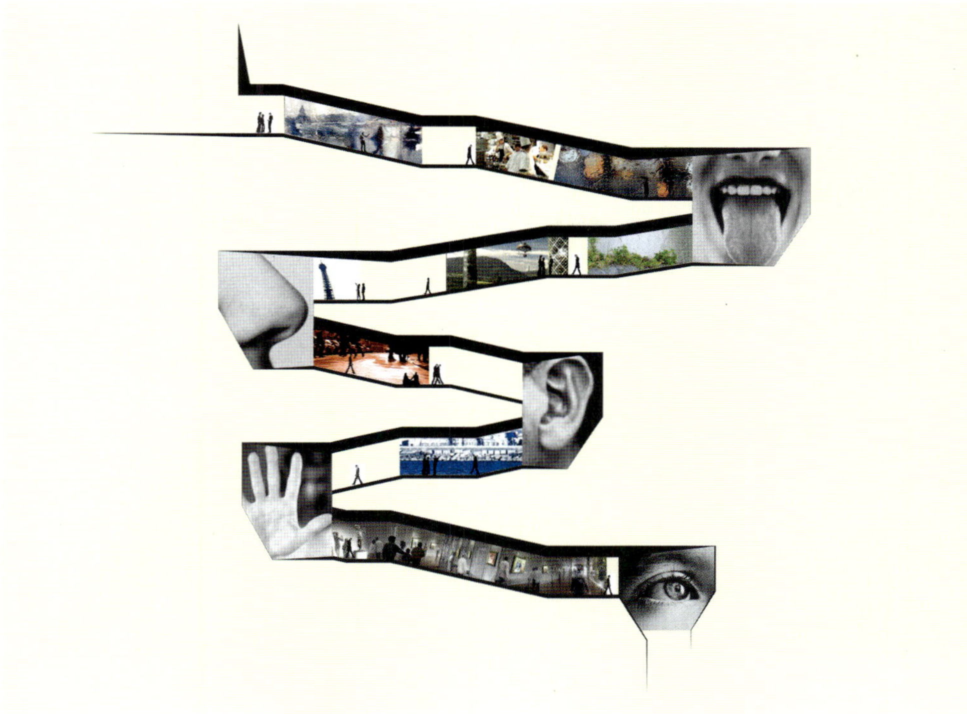

[fig. 095]

It is about conceiving cities and their architecture as variations on atmospheres, where the symbolic dimension of space is fading in favor of sense-based experiences.

[fig. 096]

[fig. 097]

[fig. 098]

[fig. 099]

Thresholds no longer occupy space as a matter of priority. Instead, they preserve metropolises' most precious capital: the body of the city dweller. As vital interstices, they enable the body to negotiate between two given engagements in the context of flows, sensory overload, and spatial challenges.

BESPOKE TAILORS
BESPOKE TAILORS
Ermenegildo Zegna
BESPOKE TAILORS
NJOUR
LOTUS BORN
BUDDHIST ART
& BOOKS
CONVEY
2739 3806
CONVEY
向前200米

[fig. 100]

Bus stand
Buses do not pick up passengers here
Paddington Station
Stand for LT services
Brixton
Oxford Circus 159
Streatham
VLA 177
205
7
Bus stand

[fig. 101]

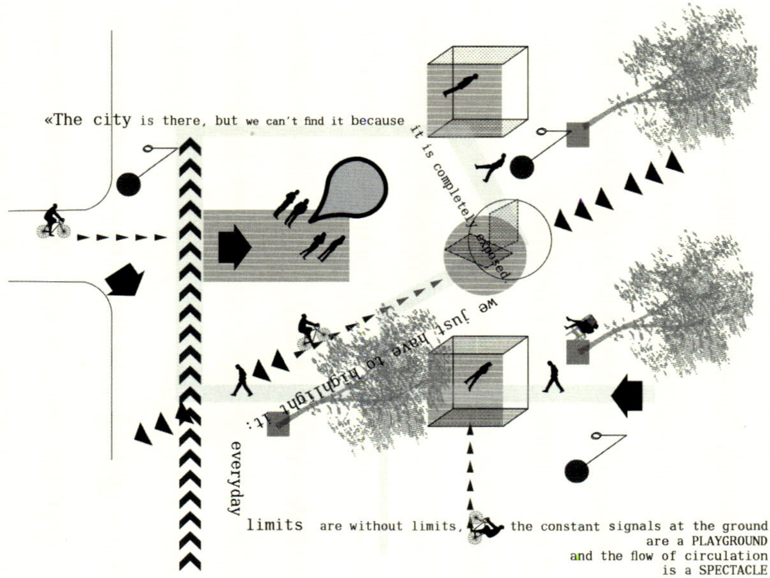
«The city is there, but we can't find it because
it is completely exposed.
we just have to highlight it:
everyday
limits are without limits, the constant signals at the ground
are a PLAYGROUND
and the flow of circulation
is a SPECTACLE

[fig. 102]

[fig. 103]

However, these new thresholds also make use of the body and the senses through their capacity to comprehend and interact with space; they open levels of perception and action.

This pleasure of being enveloped by heat as soon as you pass through Entrance 2 of the shopping center, of wandering through a uniformly balmy atmosphere, rather like getting off a plane in Cairo after having come from Paris. Forget the mud and the cold, the grayness and the traffic. Slow down, lose yourself in the gentle heat. Lose all notion of time, the passing of which no clocks show.

Annie Ernaux
Regarde les lumières mon amour

[fig. 104]

[fig. 105]

[fig. 106]

The recognition of these new thresholds opens up exciting avenues for architectural and urban design, the implementation of which now takes place within the vast spaces of contemporary developments: shopping malls, university and office campuses, leisure complexes, airports, stations... For these new thresholds, it is no longer enough to simply embody the transitions between the outside and the inside.

[fig. 107]

[fig. 108]

Instead, these new thresholds must be thought of as sequences of ambiences to be revealed—and of opportunities to be seized—with a view to tending to users' needs and accompanying them at every step of their trajectory. They must create a sense of surprise, rhythm and playfulness, enabling users to rediscover a human dimension in disembodied worlds.

[fig. 109]

[fig. 110]

[fig. 111]

[fig. 112]

By playing with fragrances, lighting, wall textures, colors, signage, screens, words, and the presence of people, new thresholds reveal and create sequences of ambiences, each offering new possibilities for experimenting with and appropriating situations.

[fig. 113]

[fig. 114]

[fig. 115]

[fig. 116]

[fig. 117]
After the closure of the fish shop, the stall becomes a local association for the inhabitants of the neighborhood.

[fig. 118]

[fig. 119]

[fig. 120]

Far from standardizing or conditioning the social and political uses of contemporary spaces, it is necessary to create sensitive and welcoming environments that open themselves up to the potential uses we might make of them—active, versatile thresholds that offer the means to transform generic spaces into true living spaces.

[fig. 121]

Humans still breathe in and out.
When is architecture going to do the same?

Aldo Van Eyck
Place and Occasion

[fig. 080]
Herman Hertzberger,
Dining in Paris

[fig. 081]
Cubicles, Pudong, China, 2016

[fig. 082]
Maasaki Miyara, *14:24 Yokohama,* from the series Urban Gardening

[fig. 083]
Naka Architects' Studio, *Apartments with a small restaurant*, Meouro, Tokyo, Japan, 2014

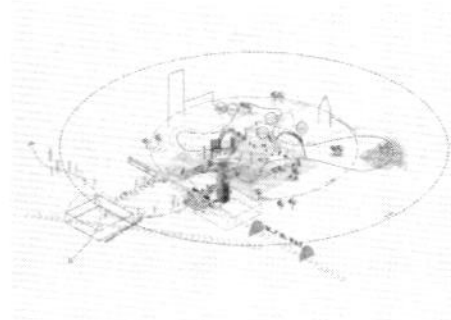

[fig. 084]
Sensual City Studio, concept drawing, *La Gare Sensuelle*, 2012

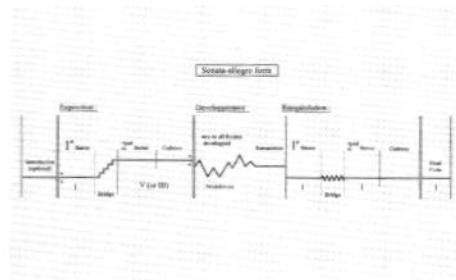

[fig. 085]
Sonata form pattern

[fig. 086]
Photogram from *North by Northwest*, directed by Alfred Hitchcock, 1959

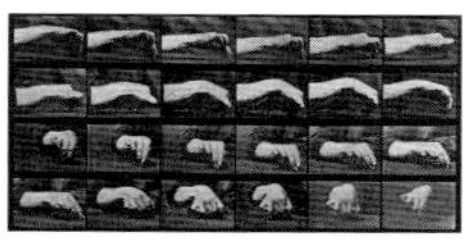

[fig. 087]
Movement of the hand, a hand drawing a circle, photogravure after Eadweard Muybridge, 1887

[fig. 088]
Photogram from *North by Northwest*, directed by Alfred Hitchcock, 1959

[fig. 089]
Marinus Boezem, *Labyrinth*, 2016, installation view at Oude Kerk, Amsterdam, Netherlands. Photo: Robert Glas.

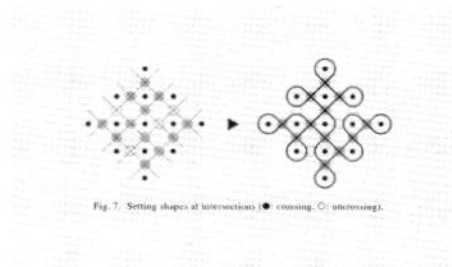

[fig. 090]
Kolam patterns study extracted from *Fundamental Study on Design System of Kolam Pattern*, 2007

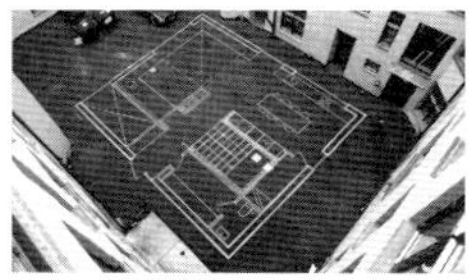

[fig. 091]
Vardehaugen, *Real scale drawing*, Stamsund, Norway

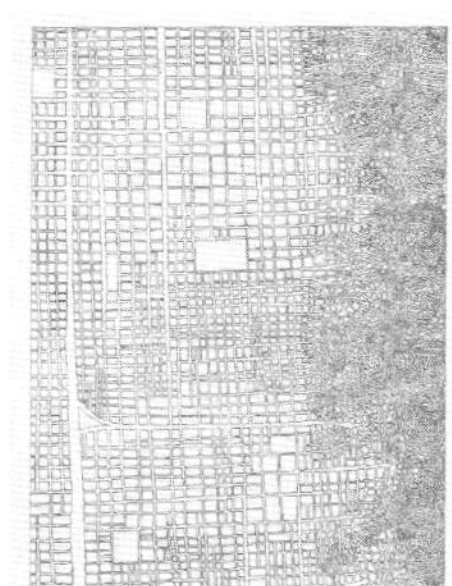

[fig. 092]
Clément Masurier, *Drawing*, May 2015

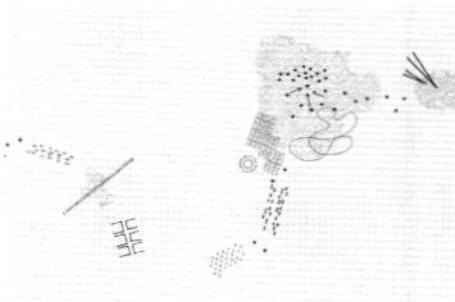

[fig. 093]
Sensual City Studio,
Mindmap, *Mindwalks*, 2016

[fig. 094]
Sensual City Studio,
competition drawing,
Lujiazui's project, 2016

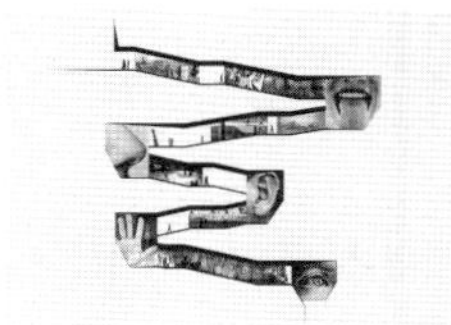

[fig. 095]
Sensual City Studio,
Le parcours de la Ville Sensuelle, French Pavillion for the Universal Exposition of Shanghai, China, 2010

[fig. 096]
Photogram from *Sun, The Sensual City Fresco*, directed by Sensual City Studio, 2010

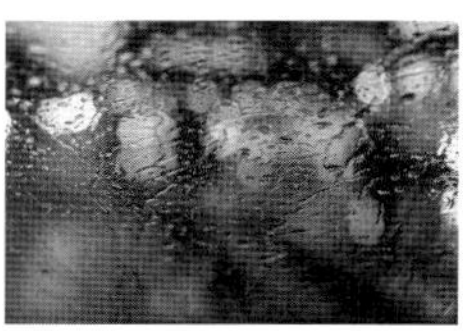

[fig. 097]
Photogram from *Rain, The Sensual City Fresco*, directed by Sensual City Studio, 2010

[fig. 098]
Crowd in a park, London, UK

[fig. 099]
Victoria Bay, Hong Kong, China

[fig. 100]
Hong Kong by night,
Hong Kong, 2008

[fig. 101]
Crowd in a street, London, UK

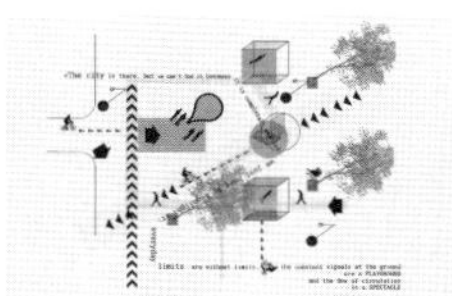

[fig. 102]
Sensual City Studio,
concept drawing,
The invisible city, 2015

[fig. 103]
Francis Kurkdjian,
installation olfactive, Paris, France, 2015—2016.

[fig. 104]
All plastic supermarket carts

[fig. 105]
Jacques Ferrier Architecture,
French Pavilion Expo 2010, Universal Exposition of Shanghai, China

[fig. 106]
Rafael Moneo,
Madrid-Atocha tropical garden, Madrid, Spain, 1991

[fig. 107]
403architecture [dajiba],
The Tower of Matsumoto,
2016

[fig. 108]
Jacques Ferrier Architecture
Air France Industries, Orly, France, 2004

[fig. 109]
Boa Mistura, *Water Ways*,
Somoto, Nicaragua, 2016

[fig. 110]
Sensual City Studio &
Jacques Ferrier Architecture,
A Path towards the Sensual City, exhibition, Aarhus, Denmark, 2017

[fig. 111]
Felice Varini, *Six ellipses pour six colonnes*, exhibition by Markus Raetz and Felice Varini, Les Halles, Porrentruy, Switzerland, 2008. Photo: André Morin

[fig. 112]
Zelin Huang/Aether Architects, *ARTINN/1*, Shenzhen, China, 2017

[fig. 113]
Jacques Ferrier Architecture, *Piper and Charles Heidsieck Headquarters*, Reims, France, 2008

[fig. 114]
Studio Pauline Marchetti & Jacques Ferrier Architecture, *International French School of Beijing*, China, 2016

[fig. 115]
Takis, *Le Bassin*, Courbevoie, Nanterre, Puteaux, France, 1988

[fig. 116]
Playground, Stockholm, Sweden, 2013

[fig. 117]
Storefront of Puesto en Construcción [PEC], Madrid, Spain

[fig. 118]
Atelier Novembre, *Le CentQuatre*, Paris, France, 2008

[fig. 119]
Sensual City Studio, *We Love Sensual City*, Paris, France, 2012

[fig. 120]
Sensual City Studio, *Climate device*, Shanghai, China, 2015

[fig. 121]
Elena Chiavi, Ahmad El Mad & Matteo Goldoni, *Antiroom II*, Valletta, Malta, 2015

Thresholds signal
to each and
every one of us

that we are
about to experience
something...

By putting the spotlight on thresholds, our work subverts the views that each of us has of architecture. In our visual narrative, the subsidiary proves to be a marker of the essential: though the threshold is by definition on *the margins*, it has nevertheless been the guiding narrative thread over time of the meaning and importance that we accord to built spaces.¶ The threshold is an extraneous space, a link that has no existence in its own right, that is outside any functional sequence; the threshold is the superfluous—*useless*—space that introduces the useful space, or which links together two *useful* spaces.

¶ It appears when symbolism comes to the fore, and disappears when functionalism triumphs in what is now globalized architecture. Rational design has eliminated thresholds. ¶ In order to find their place in situations where they feel increasingly like outsiders, contemporary men and women need thresholds, and it is only from the margins that such a renaissance—the rebirth of the threshold—can take place. These new thresholds play with meanings, temporalities, materials, lighting... Ambiences take precedence over spaces. However, just as in the past, they also assert the fundamental need to feel and experience the built environment in some way other than as a product to be consumed, and rather as the vital medium for personal and collective fulfilment. ¶ The threshold is the prism through which we call into question the way we produce space today. Crossing a threshold is not anodyne: it signals to each one of us that *we are about to experience something*. It exalts the singularity of the spaces that it serves. It is for this reason that the disappearance of thresholds—a phenomenon that has gone unnoticed—leaves all architecture bare, without relief and without substance, abandoned to its objectivity alone. ¶ Everything happens as though *the real* is falling out of our reach, as though reason is not enough to fill the void that grows every day between people and the spaces they inhabit. We have sought to personalize this observation, to bring it to life, to give it an image and a body, with a view to perhaps finding a new approach, and establishing a new contract between architecture and humanism. This personalization, the agent of our constant adaptation to situations that are beyond our control, is embodied in the threshold—that which serves no purpose and yet which is omnipresent, universal and essential. ¶ Here, we bring to light new directions for designing original thresholds that initiate ambiences and bring the experience of the body in space back to the fore. We need to reinvent

the missing threshold.

How to represent thresholds?

The disappearance of thresholds can be seen as a marker for a profound, global change in our relationship with space. Everyone feels the impoverishment in their daily urban experience. We must, then, widen our outlook and working methods to make town dwellers' experience our primary objective. The building blocks for a new life project in large cities will be atmospheres and temporality. Towns and architecture need to be rethought as a series of unique experiences. This is true if we consider the engagement of the body, notably by simply going for a stroll. This is the meaning we have given to seven walks, imagined as a story that puts thresholds at the center of our everyday focus. Our aim: to develop an original way of representing ambiances and active spaces, by offering sensory experiences as a new paradigm for cities and contemporary architecture.

Seven chronicles.

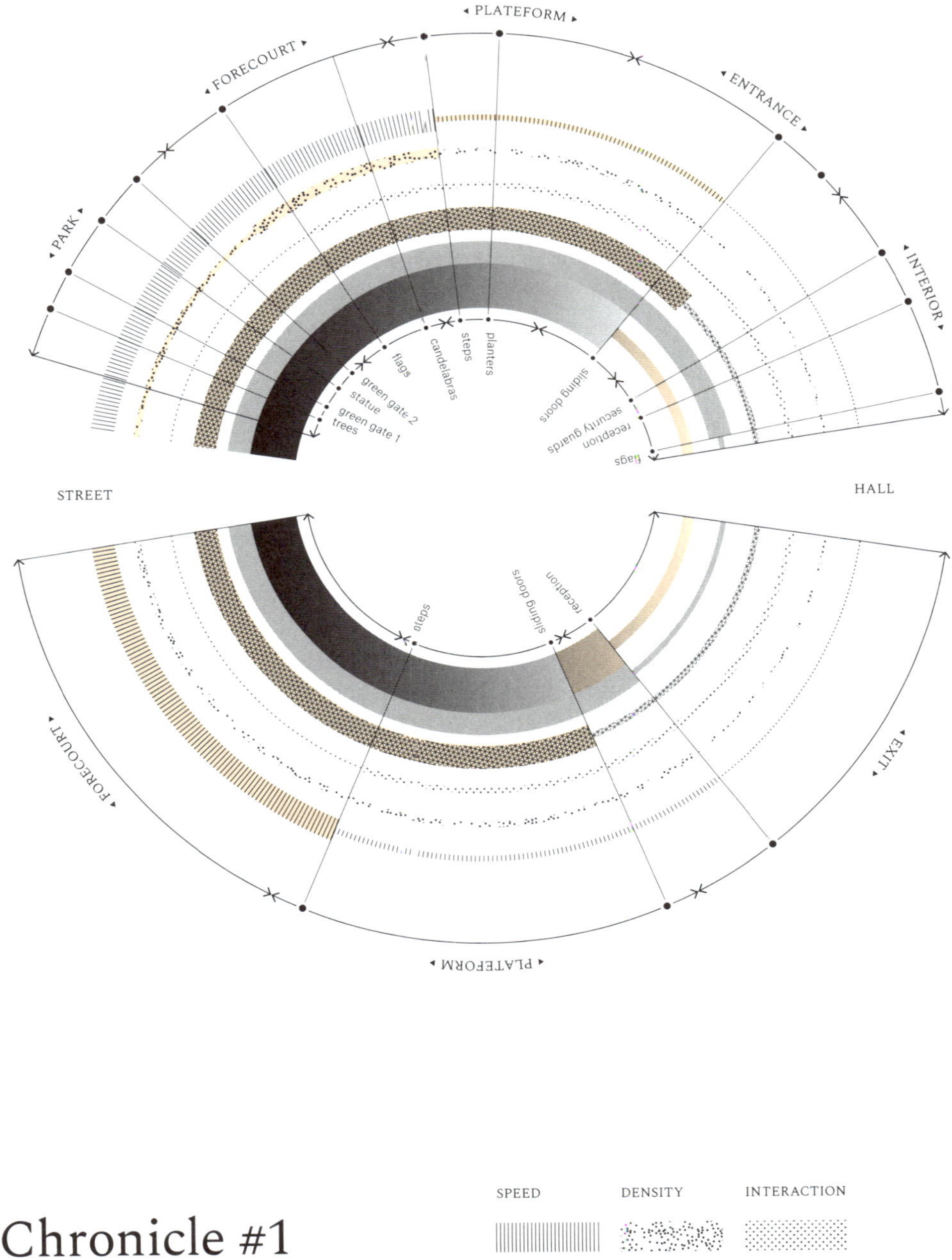
PLATEFORM
FORECOURT
ENTRANCE
PARK
INTERIOR
flags
candelabras
steps
planters
green gate 2
statue
green gate 1
trees
sliding doors
security guards
reception
flags
STREET
HALL
steps
sliding doors
reception
FORECOURT
EXIT
PLATEFORM
SPEED
DENSITY
INTERACTION

Chronicle #1

In rue Boulard, flags fly from the front of the two schools, like an initial reference point. A few public buildings are packed into the middle of Paris' 14th *arrondissement*. The web loosens to allow space for two parks which give onto rue Mouton-Duvernet on both sides. It is impossible to miss the Town Hall that pretends to hide behind the trees that follow the line of the road. In reality, the view is perfectly symmetrical, setting the stage very clearly for the weight of the institution. Having passed through a typically Parisian green gate, you reach a statue that takes centre stage in the middle of a dirt path, where children run and play ping-pong. You leave the park as quickly as you entered it, in the same way, magnetised by the size of the building.

A broad forecourt serves as a second filter. It is completely barren, and equally taken over by children running around, whose shouts replace the usual city noise. It has got everything—French and European flags on all three wings of the building, candelabras mounted at equal distances from the steps, decorated with planters, and leading to a platform that sets off the entrance. A man smokes a cigarette there. Or rather to one side, at the foot of the steps, as if this little stage is too important for him to have his break there. The facade catches the full force of the sun this early afternoon and you notice other smokers on the first-floor balcony.

In this sublime symmetry, the entrance becomes strangely peripheral. Incidentally everyone is surprised by this.

Inside, symmetry continues to rule. On the right is the reception, on the left are the first offices. Opposite is a monumental staircase with a French flag above it and stained-glass windows that subdue the light and create a muffled atmosphere inside the entrance hall where the slightest noise echoes. So, everyone whispers.

Leaving this place, the sun and the sounds of the city take over. It's as you go down the few steps of the forecourt that you realise why it is that the employee prefers to smoke his cigarette there, free from the weight of the institution.

Town Hall

SOUND WARMTH LIGHT

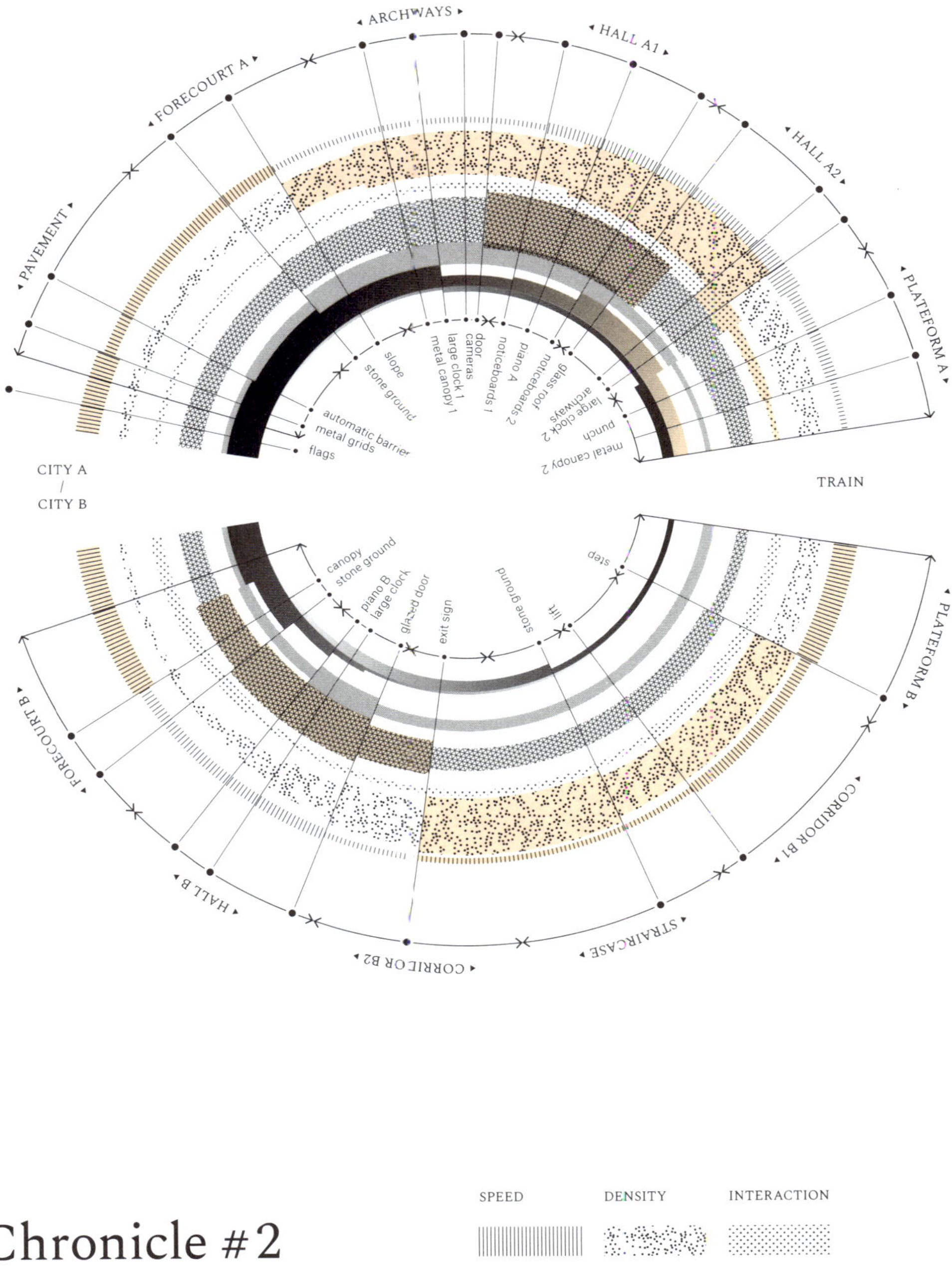
ARCHWAYS
FORECOURT A
HALL A1
HALL A2
PAVEMENT
PLATEFORM A
slope
stone ground
door
cameras
large clock 1
metal canopy 1
noticeboards 1
piano A
noticeboards 2
glass roof
archways
large clock 2
punch
metal canopy 2
automatic barrier
metal grids
flags
CITY A
/
CITY B
TRAIN
canopy
stone ground
piano B
large clock
glazed door
exit sign
stone ground
lift
step
PLATEFORM B
FORECOURT B
CORRIDOR B1
HALL B
STAIRCASE
CORRIDOR B2
SPEED
DENSITY
INTERACTION

Chronicle #2

The station is visible from a good two kilometres, like a landmark indicating the creation of the historical axis which links the north and south banks of the Seine. French flags flutter in a line across the front of the building, with a jagged, but perfectly symmetrical silhouette.

It is rare to find a building that displays the time—a large clock presides over a metal canopy under which several travellers smoke. 8.30 am, 10 minutes to departure.

We start to notice a few signs, the green cross of a pharmacy, sandwich stalls, video-surveillance cameras hidden away under the classical-looking archways that round off the staging of the intrinsic symbolism of travel. The large, wooden doors, with glazed panels reflect the capital letters fixed to the canopy: GARE DE L'EST SNCF.

Inside, everything is very un-complicated. Noticeboards indicate platform numbers in a first shopping concourse from where escalators lead down to the metro. Someone is playing the piano. We are subconsciously attracted by the natural light that comes from the second concourse, guided by another clock, which hangs from another archway. It feels cold, all of a sudden. The two side entrances let air blow in. Under the glass roof, the platforms can clearly be seen, on one level, understandable, logical, in a continuous, linear route from the centre of Paris. We punch our tickets—platform 27, carriage 14.

10.11 am.—platform 1 (since leaving Paris, it feels like it is the train that's important). Here, the platform is raised up, on a higher level. Down below, there is a long corridor, where everyone looks to the right, then to the left, before making a decision. We follow the exit sign: METZ CITY CENTRE. Sliding glass doors open onto a large hall that is plunged into semi-darkness by stained-glass windows filtering the sun light. Another pianist, another tune, another place.

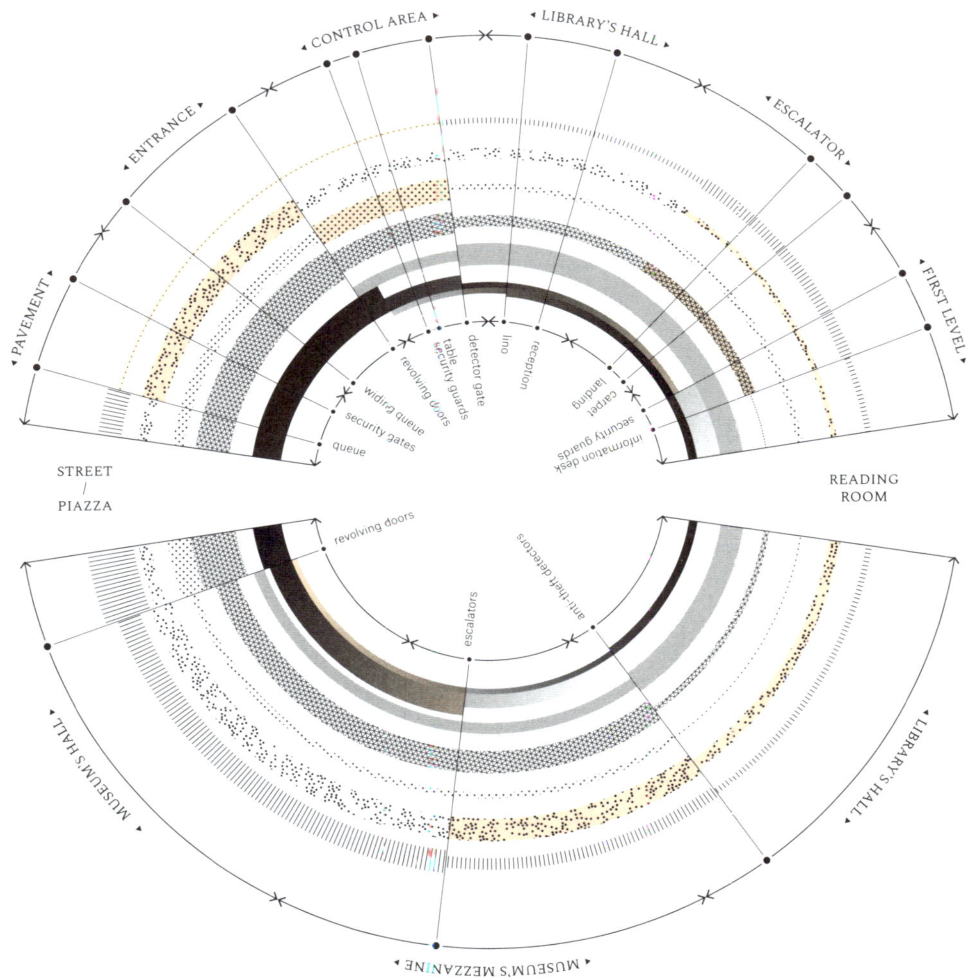

Chronicle #3

SPEED DENSITY INTERACTION

You need to be in the know. You would expect the entrance to the library to be on the museum square—not this one. It's the queue that gives it away. Hundreds of people wait in single file at the back of the building, this is where the entrance has been hidden away. It is almost invisible, hidden behind the famous blue and green pipes of the museum and the security gates blending in perfectly with this world of steel. A few tourists are even duped and wait in the queue for a few minutes, before they realise their mistake.

We take our place behind some youngsters and a few homeless people who have made the most of the free entry to spend the day in the warmth, with a book or a computer screen. After long hours spent waiting in the drizzle and wind, we are nearly there—the ever-tighter winding queue announces our imminent arrival at our destination. We are sheltered this time, but the real discomfort stems from the stench of urine and bins that hangs around the entrance to the library.

Two sets of revolving glass doors, you have to choose. Right or left, one or the other, but it matters little as the ritual is the same. A security guard on each side, sitting at a small table where bags and personal objects must be placed and then slid past, before you go through a metal detector gate to collect everything—just like an airport.

Once inside, there is not a soul. The escalator in the grand entrance hall invites us to go up to the first level. We now realise where everyone has disappeared to. There are almost as many people as there are books in the silent expanse that is the reading room. It emits an ambiance of reassurance, solemn but accessible. The natural light has reasserted itself and tranquilly radiates across the worktables.

When it is time to leave the library, we emerge rather oddly into the museum's mezzanine. A few anti-theft detectors protect the premises—nothing should leave by these doors. Except for the silence. We are met with the noise of visitors and we end up leaving the museum at the exact place where we thought we would have found the library—by those very familiar revolving doors on the Pompidou Centre piazza.

Library

SOUND WARMTH LIGHT

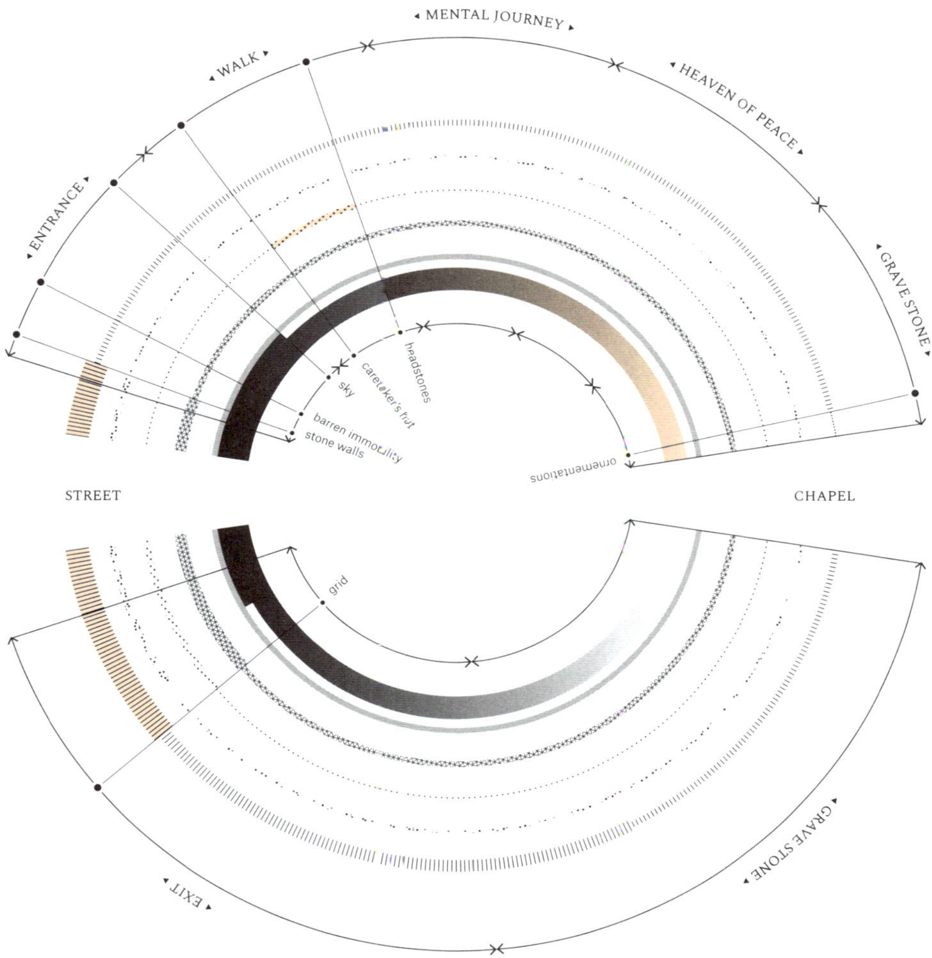
MENTAL JOURNEY
WALK
HEAVEN OF PEACE
ENTRANCE
GRAVE STONE
headstones
caretaker's hut
sky
barren immobility
stone walls
ornementations
STREET
CHAPEL
grid
GRAVE STONE
EXIT

Chronicle #4

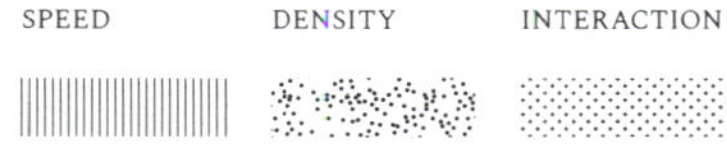
SPEED
DENSITY
INTERACTION

A little haven of peace is revealed once you enter the cemetery walls. The sun is dazzling—after the shade of the street, the sky opens up. The recumbent, solemn grave stones appear in an arrangement marked by perspective. Everything seems ordered, numb. This passage away from urban life to this barren immobility surprises us, transports us.

We hesitate before starting on our serene stroll, torn between the feeling of desecrating this sanctuary with our footsteps and the desire to plunge into this unique tranquillity. The caretaker's hut reminds us that when we enter this place we are not completely free to do as we like, it is a protected enclave, somewhere to be respected. Once we have entered, we maintain a level of decorum in our way of walking, our way of talking.

To enter the cemetery boundary, is to leave the profane for the sacred—the realm of the dead belongs to a space outside the ordinary, the commonplace. It is a mental and symbolic journey that translates this experience into a meaningful gateway that goes beyond urban fluidity.

Passing through the cemetery gate takes us back to our most private place. The uniqueness of each headstone engraved with a name and familiar epitaphs, of these funerary chapels, singular in their decoration, contrast with the anonymity of the road beyond the cemetery boundary. The wall stands as protector of these fragments of intimacy, it delimits the closed yet communal place. It is this paradox that makes the experience of crossing it quite unique. A further idea of the world that exposes its frontiers—rejection of the cult of transparency that supposes attention must slide towards function, the abstract without pausing on outside appearances.

Here, what is inside does not open itself to the outside, to the democratic rule of the street, while light and movement from outside create no disruption inside the boundary. Each world shows its own distinct speciality and whoever passes from one to the other grasps all it has to offer.

SOUND WARMTH LIGHT

Cemetery

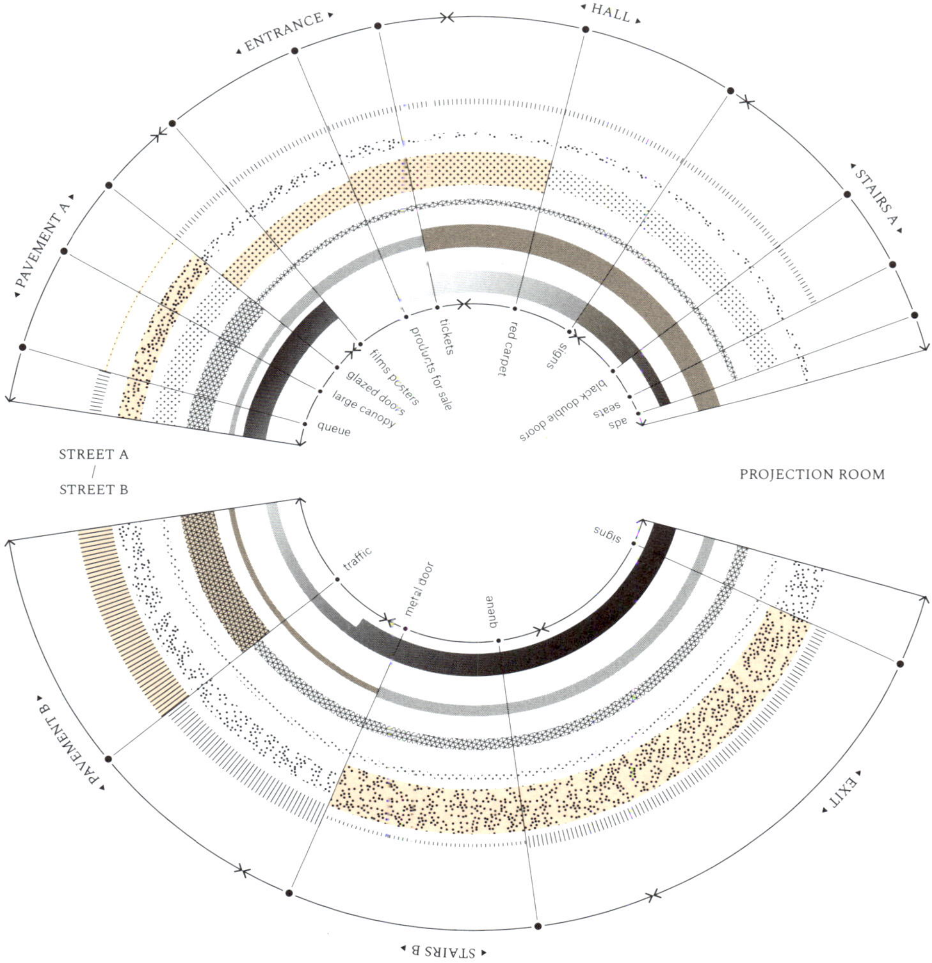

Chronicle #5

SPEED DENSITY INTERACTION

The queue of filmgoers engulfs the pavement where a large canopy announces the entrance and offers shelter against the rain. Once through the glazed doors, it's warm inside, the atmosphere muffled. Yet the lights remain quite intense—the spotlights showcase the movie posters and products for sale.

We get a ticket for the next film, then explore the entrance hall, enveloped in the red carpet and black walls, while we wait for the screening. The smell of popcorn draws us towards the counter where sweets and drinks are on offer. We look for the door to our auditorium or at least a sign for it. Then, following the general hubbub, the crowd goes up the stairs to reach the black double doors.

The lighting becomes more and more subdued as we enter the auditorium—looking around, we get an idea of the room's layout, size and the number of seats that are still free. We take off our coats and make ourselves comfortable in the wide, red armchairs, while we absentmindedly watch the ads. It suddenly becomes dark and conversations fade. Then they stop completely—the film starts.

The movie is over. A small, soft light tells us that we must leave by the doors with the twinkling, green EXIT sign. We go out in a single file via a narrow staircase that leads to a metal door. This opens abruptly onto the outside. We become aware of the town that we had forgotten for two hours—daylight or darkness, heat or cold, contrasting with the mild room, the traffic noise. We come out on rue du Cher and have lost our bearings.

Cinema

SOUND WARMTH LIGHT

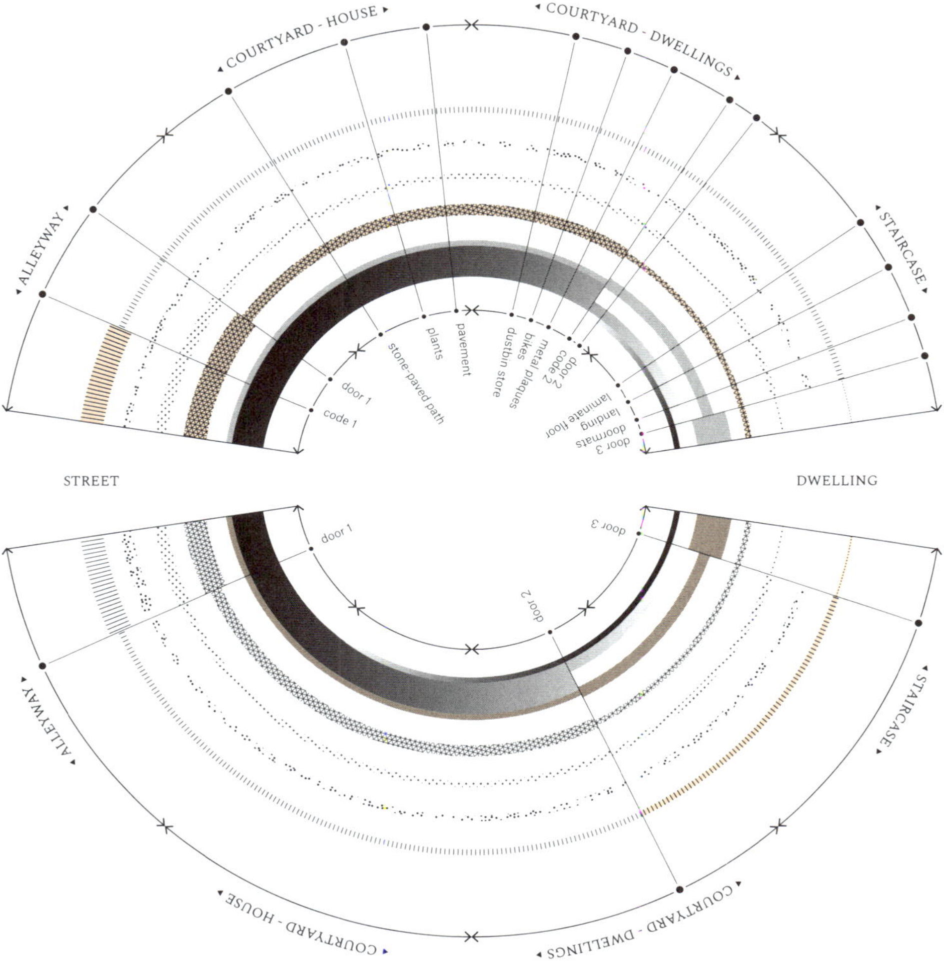

Chronicle #6

SPEED DENSITY INTERACTION

The Vélib bike-sharing station is not far away. Actually, it is just opposite. You can even hear the beep as the red changes to green as you arrive at the gate—it breaks up the linearity of the fronts of the buildings along the road. Wedged in and creating a gap between a well-to-do house and a more standard-sized building, it allows you to separate out the unexpected alleyway from the rather dense fabric of rue Froidevaux.

Entry code: 85437. The heavy door opens onto a stonepaved path, wide enough to let a car through. There is a kind of long courtyard with a fairly low building with a tiled roof at the end. The noise of the road is toned down as you go in, and the stench of exhausts gives way to the scent of plants. Miniscule pavements, completely superfluous given the entirely pedestrian nature of the place, lead to the dustbin store, which adjoins the house's garden.

The outline of the house accentuates the variety of shapes that are at the heart of this cluster of houses. All of it is very well-kept and gives off an almost rustic atmosphere. The trees, bicycles and pushchairs in disarray, a few metal plaques announce this or that profession within the collective dwelling. We have left Paris.

The door that is of interest to us—reached by two small, stone steps—requires a second code: 78941. We are met with a gloomy, narrow, steep staircase that leads to the first floor, where three doormats lie in front of only two doors. The one on the right leads to an apartment. White parquet runs through the two rooms whose wide windows overlook the stone path that we have just left. A cocoon protected from the noise of the city.

As night falls, the courtyard is not lit. To leave, it is the same refrain, but in reverse. A sequence where you carry out the same everyday actions—holding doors, saying hello and thank you and using codes learnt off by heart.

SOUND WARMTH LIGHT

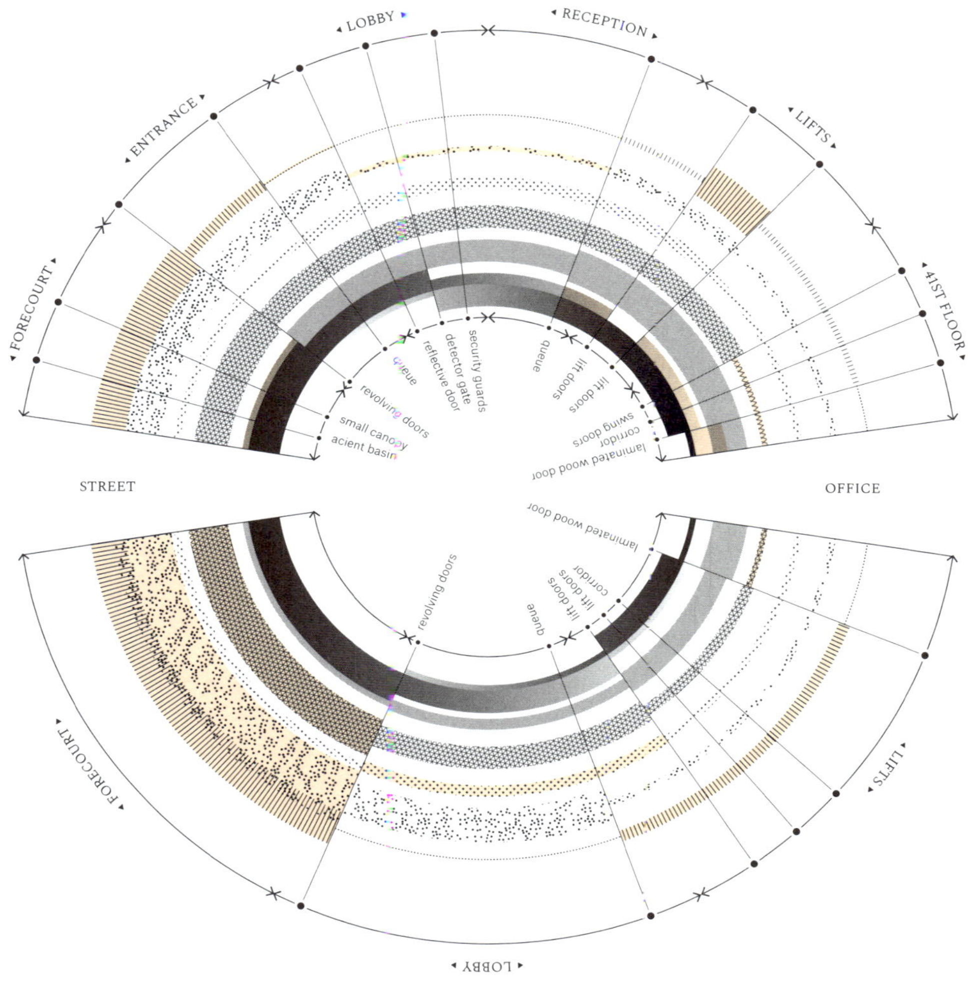

FORECOURT
ENTRANCE
LOBBY
RECEPTION
LIFTS
41ST FLOOR
STREET
OFFICE
acient basin
small canopy
revolving doors
queue
reflective door
detector gate
security guards
queue
lift doors
lift doors
swing doors
corridor
laminated wood door
laminated wood door
corridor
lift doors
lift doors
queue
revolving doors
FORECOURT
LOBBY
LIFTS

Chronicle #7

SPEED
DENSITY
INTERACTION

To stand at the foot of the tower, jammed between the fast roads that surround it and its own overwhelming verticality, is a unique experience. A few smokers shiver, frozen by the biting wind, aggravated by the movement of people entering and leaving. We can just make out the traces of the ancient basin that encircles the building, water must have run along these mosaic tiles, but it is now dry and empty. No longer any room for this fluid, living element—barrenness rules over the forecourt.

A small canopy—hardly deep enough to shelter from the rain—marks the entrance. It is flanked by four revolving doors projecting from the façade. We feel small, really small. We join the short queue and then go inside. The wind gives way to solemnity and control, in a double-height lobby with a reflective floor and electric spotlights that lend a feel of an outdated hotel. Vigipirate, government security—the controls reinforce the feeling of austerity, where some tourists, who have come to visit the panoramic roof, mix with the suits and heels of employees who work at the several companies operating from the building. We take the first lift that arrives. To the 41st floor.

The ascent is quite fast, the doors open onto a generous, garishly lit floor. Swing doors on all sides lead to a set of offices, which are carefully arranged along a corridor that encircles the central core of the building. Inside one of them, after pushing through the laminated wood door, Paris appears suddenly beyond the glass façade. A remarkable view, in complete contrast to the feeling of smallness we felt at the base. A feeling that is quickly rediscovered once the journey is repeated in the other direction. Outside, the wind is getting stronger and stronger.

Tower

SOUND WARMTH LIGHT

Selected bibliography

Alloa, Emmanuel. 2008. "Architectures de la transparence", Appareil [En ligne], 1, URL: http://appareil.revues.org/138; DOI: 10.4000/appareil.138

Augé, Marc. 1992. *Non-Lieux, introduction à une anthropologie de la surmodernité*. Paris: Seuil.

Aviolat, Alexandre, Christophe Joud. 2015. "L'univers domestique de la pièce". In *Matières*, N°12, pp. 85—94.

Arendt, Hannah. 1958. *The Human Condition*. London & Chicago: University of Chicago Press.

Asimov, Isaac. 1951. *Foundation*. New York: Gnome Press.

Bachelard, Gaston. 1961 (1957). *La poétique de l'espace*. Paris: Presses Universitaires de France.

Banham, Reyner. 1984. *The Architecture of the Well-tempered Environment*. Chicago: University of Chicago Press.

Barberger, Nathalie. 2011. *Pensées de passage*. Villeneuve-d'Ascq: Presses Universitaires du Septentrion.

Baudelaire, Charles. 1933. *Petits poèmes en prose*. Paris: Javal et Bourdeau.

Bauman, Zygmund. 2000. *Liquid Modernity*. Cambridge: Polity Press.

Benjamin, Walter. 1972. "Erfahrung und Armut" (1933). In *Gesammelte Schriften (II.1)*. Frankfurt a. M.: Suhrkamp. pp. 213—219.

Benjamin, Walter. 1982. *Passagenwerk, vol.1*. Frankfurt a. M.: Suhrkamp.

Berger, John. 1972. *Ways of Seeing*. London: Penguin Books.

Boettger, Till. 2014. *Thresholds Spaces: Transitions in Architecture. Analysis and Design tools*. Basel: Birkhäuser.

Bonnin, Philippe, Roselyne de Villanova (Eds.). 2006. *Loges, concierges & gardiens; enquêtes en Europe: Paris, Londres, Barcelone, Milan, Oslo*. Paris: Créaphis.

Bonnin, Philippe, Jacques Pezeu-Massabuau. 2017. *Façons d'habiter au Japon. Maisons, villes et seuils*. Paris: CNRS Éditions.

Chanvillard, Cécile. 2011. *Au seuil de l'architecture le sacré*. Louvain: Laboratoire Architecture Analyse. Faculté d'architecture, d'ingénierie architecturale, d'urbanisme.

Coles, Alex (Ed.). 2016. *EP Vol.2— Design Fiction*. Berlin: Sternberg Press.

Coupland, Douglas. 1994. *Life After God*. New York: Pocket Books.

Debray, Régis. 2010. Éloge des frontières. Paris: Gallimard.

De Certeau, Michel. 1990 (1980). *L'Invention du quotidien, 1.: Arts de faire*. Paris: Gallimard.

Dibie, Pascal. 2012. *Ethnologie de la porte. Des passages et des seuils.* Paris: Métailié.

Di Palma, Vittoria, Diana Periton, Marina Lathouri. 2008. *Intimate Metropolis: Urban Subjects in the Modern City*. London: Routledge.

Doxiadis, Constantinos Apostolou. 1968. *Ekistics: An Introduction to the Science of Human Settlements.* New York: Oxford University Press.

Eleb, Monique, Anne Debarre. 1995. *L'invention de l'habitation moderne, Paris 1880—1914*. Paris: Hazan.

Eleb, Monique, Anne Debarre. 1999. *Architectures de la vie privée: maisons et mentalités, XVIIe—XIXe siècles, Volume 1*. Paris: Hazan.

Ernaux, Annie. 2016. *Regarde les lumières mon amour*. Paris: Gallimard.

Foucault, Michel. 1984. "Des espaces autres, Dits et écrits 1984". In *Architecture, Mouvement, Continuité*. N°5, pp. 46—49.

Gabestan, Jean-François. 2004. *La conquête du plain-pied. L'immeuble à Paris au XVIIIe siècle*. Paris: Picard.

Gaudin, Henri. 2004. *Seuil et d'ailleurs: texte, croquis, dessins.* Besançon: Editions de l'Imprimeur.

Geist, Johann Friedrich. 1985. *Arcades: The History of a Building Type*. Cambridge, Mass.: MIT Press.

Gibson, James J. 1950. *The Perception of the Visual World*. Cambridge: The Riverside Press.

Grumbach, Antoine. 2007. *L'ombre, le seuil, la limite. Réflexions sur l'espace juif*. Paris: Musée d'art et d'histoire du Judaïsme.

Hamon, Philippe. 1989. *Expositions: littérature et architecture au XIXe siècle*. Paris: Corti.

Hertzberger, Herman. 2005 (1991). *Lessons for students in architecture.* Rotterdam: NAI010 Publishers.

Karnchaonaoirn, Nuttinee. 2016. "Ambigous Threshold". In *Harvard Design Magazine*, N°42, p. 207.

Koyré, Alexandre. 1968 (1957). *From the Close World to the Infinite Universe*. Baltimore: Johns Hopkins University Press.

Lussault, Michel, Jacques Lévy (Eds.). 2003. *Dictionnaire de la géographie et de l'espace des sociétés*. Paris: Belin.

Lussault, Michel. 2013. *L'avènement du monde. Essai sur l'habitation humaine de la terre*. Paris: Seuil.

Merleau-Ponty, Maurice. 1945. *Phénoménologie de la perception.* Paris: La Librairie Gallimard, NRF.

Moley, Christian. 2003. *Entre ville et logement en quête d'espaces intermédiaires.* Paris: ENSA Paris La Villette.

Mongin, Olivier. 2013. *La ville des flux.* Paris: Fayard.

Mukherji, Subha. 2011. *Thinking on Thresholds: The Poetics of Transitive Spaces.* London: Anthem Press.

Norberg-Schulz, Christian. 1975. *Meaning in Western Architecture.* Santa Barbara, Ca.: Praeger.

Norberg-Schulz, Christian. 1981. *Genius Loci.* Bruxelles: Mardaga.

Pallasmaa, Juhani. 2005. *The Eyes of the Skin: Architecture and the Senses.* Hoboken, NJ: John Wiley & Sons.

Perec, Georges. 2008 (1974). *Species of Spaces and Other Pieces.* London: Penguin Books.

Rasmussen, Steen Eiler. 1959. *Experiencing Architecture.* Cambridge, Mass.: MIT Press.

Sansot, Pierre. 2008. *Rêveries dans la ville.* Paris: Carnets Nord.

Scheerbart, Paul. 1972 (1914). *Glass Architecture.* New York, Washington: Praeger Publishers.

Schmitt, Jean-Claude. 2013. "Le seuil et la porte". In Boucheron, Patrick, Jean- Philippe Genet (Eds.). *Marquer la ville. Signes, traces et empruntes du pouvoir.* Paris, Rome: Éditions de la Sorbonne, École française de Rome.

Scully, Vincent. 2013 (1969). *The Earth, the Temple, and the Gods: Greek Sacred Architecture.* San Antonio: Trinity University Press.

Sennett, Richard. 1991. *The Conscience of the Eye: The design and social life of cities.* London: Faber and Faber.

Serfaty-Garzon, Perla. 2003 "Le Chez-soi: habitat et intimité". In Segaud, Marion, Jacques Brun, Jean-Claude Driant (Eds.). *Dictionnaire critique de l'habitat et du logement.* Paris: Editions Armand Colin.

Sloterdijk, Peter. 2004. *Shären III. Schäume.* Berlin: Suhrkamp.

de la Soudière, Martin (Ed.). 2000. *Communications,* N°70, Seuils, passages.

Soulier, Nicolas. 2012. *Reconquérir les rues. Exemples à travers le monde et pistes d'action.* Paris: Ulmer.

Stavrides, Stavros. 2010. *Towards the City of Thresholds.* Trento: Professionaldreamers.

Taut, Bruno. 1972 (1917). *Alpine Architecture.* New York, Washington: Praeger Publishers.

Teyssot, Georges. 2013.
A Topology of Everyday Constellations.
Cambridge, Mass.: MIT Press.

Thibaud, Jean-Paul, Cristine
Rose Duarte. 2013. *Ambiances urbaines en partage: Pour une écologie sociale de la ville sensible.* Genève: MétisPresses.

Thibaud, Jean-Paul. 2015.
En quête d'ambiances: Éprouver la ville en passant. Genève: MétisPresses.

Turner, Victor. 1977. *The Ritual Process.*
Ithaca: Cornell University Press.

Van Eyck, Arnold. "Place and occasion".
In Litgelijn, Vincent, Francis Strauven (Eds.). 2008. *Aldo Van Eyck: Collected Articles and Other Writings, 1947-1998.*
Amsterdam: Sun Publishers.

Van Gennep, Arnold. 1960.
The Rites of Passage. London: Routledge and Kegan Paul.

Webber, Melvin M. 1996 (1994).
L'urbain sans lieu ni bornes.
Paris: Ed. de l'Aube.

Image credits

1 © Lars Lovøld, Rainforest Foundation Norway
2 © flickr user: Will Art photo under CC BY 2.0
3 © flickr user: Rachel Harmon photo under CC BY 2.0
4 © flickr user: Seier+Seier photo under CC BY-SA 2.0
5 © flickr user: xlibber - CC
6 © Collection Frac Centre-Val de Loire, Donation Ettore Sottsass
7 © Wikipedia user: Bernard Gagnon photo under CC BY-SA 3.0
11 © Superstudio
12 © Wikipedia user: Henley Quadling, photo under CC BY-SA 3.0
14 All rights reserved
18 © Photo by Tim Clayton Corbis via Getty Images
19 © flickr user: Eduard Marmet photo under CC BY-SA 2.0
22 © Nuttinee Karnchanaporn
23 © Wikipedia user: Wouter Hagens photo under CC-BY-SA-3.0
24 © Wikipedia user: 663highland photo under CC BY 2.5
25 © Wikipedia user: Djampa photo under CC BY-SA 4.0, 3.0
27 © flickr used: Lars Plougmann photo under CC BY-SA 2.0
28 © Wikipedia user: Velvet photo under CC BY-SA 4.0
29 © flickr user: Gunnar Klack photo under CC BY-SA 2.0
30 © flickr user: Molly Adams photo under CC BY 2.0
31 © flickr user: Marlytyz photo under CC BY 2.0
32 © Richard C. Anderson
33 © SCS/Estefania Mompean
35 © Myr Muratet
36 © Lia Nalbantidou/Studiotessera from the series "The Secure, Private Domain of my Home (1996-2001) – Zero to Five"
38 © flickr user: Denna Jones photo under CC BY 2.0
39 © SCS/Elisa Alvarez
41 © Wikipedia user: Starus photo under CC BY-SA 3.0
42 All rights reserved
43 © flickr user: Paul Townsend photo under CC BY-SA 2.0
46 © flickr user: IK's World Trip photo under CC BY 2.0
47 © flickr user: Nelson Minar photo under CC BY-SA 2.0
48 © flickr user: NCDOTcommunications, photo under CC BY 2.0
55 © flickr user: Michael photo under CC BY 2.0
56 © Wikipedia user: DC photo under CC BY-SA 3.0,
57 © flickr user: Dan4th Nicholas photo under CC BY 2.0
58 © flickr user: William Murphy photo under CC BY-SA 2.0
59 © flickr user: Mark B. Schlemmer, photo under CC BY 2.0
60 © SCS
61 © flickr user: Chris Marchant photo under CC BY 2.0
63 © Pipilotti Rist. Courtesy of the artist, Hauser & Wirth and Luhring Augustine
64 © flickr user: Peter Dutton, photo under CC BY 2.0
65 © Alberto Giuliani
66 © Lordprice Collection Alamy Stock Photo
68 © SCS/Pauline Marchetti
69 © flickr user: Ben Tesch, photo under CC BY 2.0

70 © flickr user: Matthew W. Jackson photo under CC BY-SA 2.0
71 © flickr user: Takashi Hososhima photo under CC BY-SA 2.0
73 © Constantinos and Emma Doxiadis Foundation
74 © flickr user: N i c o l a photo under CC BY 2.0
75 © SCS/Pauline Marchetti
76 © Design Pics Inc Alamy Stock Photo
77 © flickr user: Tinou Bao photo under CC BY 2.0
78 © flickr user: Tony Hisgett photo under CC BY 2.0
81 © INDG 2016
82 © Wikipedia user: Marc Mongenet photo under CC BY-SA 4.0
83 © flickr user: Andrew Pilloud photo under CC BY 2.0
84 © Aram Bartholl
85 © flickr user: Gesa Henselmans photo under CC BY 2.0
86 © flickr user: Seattle Municipal Archives, photo under CC BY 2.0
87 © Nicole Starosielski
88 © Barcelona Supercomputing Center
89 © Space Popular, Lara Lesmes & Fredrik Hellberg
97 © Herman Herzberger
98 © SCS/Estefania Mompean
99 © Masaaki Miyara and Argyle Design Limited. www.argyledesign.co.jp
100 © Naka Architects' Studio
101 © SCS
106 © Marinus Boezem photo by Robert Glas
109 © Vardehaugen www.vardehaugen.no
110 © Clément Masurier
111 © SCS
112 © SCS
113 © SCS
116 © flickr user: Alan Stanton
117 © flickr user: Bernard Spragg. NZ public domain
118 © SCS/Pauline Marchetti
119 © flickr user: CGP Grey photo under CC BY 2.0
120 © SCS
121 © Francis Kurkdjian
123 © flickr user: Polycart photo under CC BY 2.0
124 © Luc Boegly
125 © Javier Alvarez
126 All right reserved 403architecture photo by kentahasegawa
127 © Jean-Marie Monthier
128 © Boa Mistura
129 © SCS/Pauline Marchetti
130 © Felice Varini
131 © Zelin Huang/Aether Architects
132 © André Morin
133 © Luc Boegly
134 All right reserved
135 © SCS/Estefania Mompean
136 © Adriana Martínez. 2018
137 © SCS/Clémentin Rachet
138 © SCS/Jacques Ferrier
139 © Eiichi Kano
140 © Elena Chiavi, Ahmad El Mad & Matteo Goldoni

Pauline Marchetti
is a DPLG certified architect and a graduate of the École Nationale Supérieure d'Architecture de Paris-Belleville. She led with Jacques Ferrier the French Pavilion project for the World Expo 2010 of Shanghai. Among other things, she is seeking to develop a design and production method based on the sensory and humanist dimension of space (volume, materiality, light, moods). In 2016, she created her architecture firm, Studio Pauline Marchetti, to implement ideas and plans devised within Sensual City Studio. She is a professor at the École Nationale Supérieure des Arts Décoratifs de Paris.

Estefania Mompean
is an urban designer and architect who graduated from the Universidad de Alicante. She received a bursary from the Fundación Arquia del Colegio Oficial de Arquitectos in Spain for her academic career. She is committed to the exploration of urban development from her research at the Why Factory at TUDelft University. She has been developing a conceptual vision for the Sensual City Studio since 2011, actively participating in international urban projects, architecture, design and installations.

Philippe Simay
is a philosopher. After completing his PhD in philosophy, his research has focused on the history of human and social sciences within the framework of an attachment with the Social Anthropology Laboratory (Collège de France in Paris), political sciences (the Maison Française in Oxford) and esthetics (Terra Foundation of Chicago). Formerly Programme Director at the Collège International de Philosophie, he has been involved in the work of Sensual City Studio since 2011.
He is a professor at the Ecole Nationale Supérieure d'Architecture de Paris-Belleville and travels all around the world for the documentary series *Habiter le Monde* (Arte).

Jacques Ferrier
is an architect and urban planner. Following his architectural training at the École Nationale Supérieure d'Architecture de Paris-Belleville and the École Centrale de Paris, he created his own architecture firm in Paris in 1993. His portfolio of work includes cultural and leisure facilities, showcase buildings and public buildings. He is the author of a number of books and articles. His work has been the subject of many publications, exhibitions and has been the recipient of a number of prizes and awards in France and abroad.

The Sensual City Studio (SCS) was conceived as a place for reflection where time is taken to formulate and develop thoughts—a long journey vital to the process of designing and realizing projects. Approaching space in all its physical, sociological and symbolic complexity is only possible when there is a decompartmentalization of disciplines and a spirit of collaboration—something reflected in the composition of the Studio's team, which includes architects, designers, a philosopher, and a geographer. This cluster of contributors, at the intersection of knowledge and creation, brings together different perspectives, visions and outlooks: an open approach based on coconstruction that enriches our understanding of the challenges and issues at stake, and gives meaning and a strong guiding narrative to the realization of the projects undertaken by SCS. This stance, which places values on research and in-depth comprehension, concurs with the humanist tradition of the studio as a place for study where, as in the Renaissance era, the arts and the sciences converge and benefit mutually from their respective contributions.

Our aim is to offer a more sensitive angle from which to view architecture and the city: instead of simply highlighting the potential of technical solutions, we want to put people back at the heart of our projects. To achieve this, we take emotions and sensations seriously, as all too often they have been ignored and sometimes mistreated in contemporary cities.

The various facets of a multisensory approach—for example, introducing a sensitive and sensory dimension to the way we represent things, transcribing ambiences and atmospheres, conveying the quality of light and materials, constructing a project imaginary—enable us to reveal architecture by calling upon different senses and drawing inspiration from real-life experiences. This subjective aspect of the perception of ambiences brings with it a form of questioning about the representation of this perception: how can an architect show what cannot be seen but only felt? It is this thinking that underlies the production of graphic and audiovisual documents within the Studio. We seek to appeal to the sensitivity and sensibilities of our interlocutors by giving free rein to imagination and personal interpretation, enabling us to conceive not just of the visible, but also of what is perceived and felt within a given space.

The editor and publisher would like to thank image rights holders who have kindly given their permission for publication. Every effort has been made to identify all rights holders before publication. We would ask any rights holders we did not manage to contact to get in touch with the editor. This project would not have been possible without the precious advices of Javier Àlvarez, Giuseppe Carleo and Hélène Bechet.

Acknowledgments

Imprint notice

Concept, drawings, texts,
and graphic design
by Sensual City Studio

Pauline Marchetti
Jacques Ferrier
Philippe Simay
Estefania Mompean
+
Elisa Àlvarez
François Gastesoleil
Fabien Goutelle
Clémentin Rachet
Mathilde Van Steenkiste

www.sensual-city.com
www.search.sensual-city.com

Cover
Sensual City Studio

Design and setting
Sensual City Studio

Translations
Oliver Waine
Beth McMillan Lownds

Proofreading
Lynne Kolar-Thompson

Lithography
Bild1 Druck, Berlin

Printed in the European Union

Bibliographic information published by the Deutsche Nationalbibliothek
The Deutsche Nationalbibliothek lists this publication in the Deutsche Nationalbibliografie; detailed bibliographic data are available on the Internet at http://dnb.d-nb.de

jovis Verlag GmbH
Kurfürstenstraße 15/16
10785 Berlin

www.jovis.de

jovis books are available worldwide in select bookstores. Please contact your nearest bookseller or visit www. jovis.de for information concerning your local distribution.

ISBN
978-3-86859-520-8